Hear Here!

Practical Listening Skills in Real-Life Situations

Anthony Allan

Australia · Brazil · Mexico · Singapore · United Kingdom · United States

Hear Here!—Practical Listening Skills in Real-Life Situations

Anthony Allan

© 2024 Cengage Learning K.K.

ALL RIGHTS RESERVED. No part of this work covered by the copyright herein may be reproduced, transmitted, stored, or used in any form or by any means—graphic, electronic, or mechanical, including but not limited to photocopying, recording, scanning, digitizing, taping, Web distribution, information networks, or information storage and retrieval systems—without the prior written permission of the publisher.

"National Geographic", "National Geographic Society" and the Yellow Border Design are registered trademarks of the National Geographic Society ® Marcas Registradas

Photo Credits:
cover: © View Pictures/Universal Images Group/Getty Image; 4: © stock adobe.com; 5: © stock adobe.com; 11: © stock adobe.com; 13: © stock adobe.com; 14: © stock adobe.com; 17: © stock adobe.com; 20: © stock adobe.com; 23: © stock adobe.com; 25: (1) © Paolo Bona/Shutterstock.com, (2) © iStock.com/Grafissimo, (3) © Shutterstock.com, (4) © Nadezda Murmakova/Shutterstock.com, (5) © Alessia Pierdomenico/Shutterstock.com; 28: © stock adobe.com; 29: © stock adobe.com; 32: © iStock.com/sturti; 33: © stock adobe.com; 35: © stock adobe.com; 36: © stock adobe.com; 38: © stock adobe.com; 39: © Celso Pupo Rodrigues | Dreamstime.com; 41: © stock adobe.com; 47: © stock adobe.com; 50: © stock adobe.com; 53: © stock adobe.com; 54: © stock adobe.com; 55:© stock adobe.com; 59: © stock adobe.com; 65: © stock adobe.com; 66: © iStock.com/Jacob Wackerhausen; 71: © stock adobe.com; 73: © stock adobe.com; 77: © stock adobe.com; 80: © Lawrey - stock.adobe.com; 83: © stock adobe.com; 87: © stock adobe.com; 89: © stock adobe.com;

For permission to use material from this textbook or product, e-mail to **eltjapan@cengage.com**

ISBN: 978-4-86312-428-8

National Geographic Learning | Cengage Learning K.K.
No. 2 Funato Building 5th Floor
1-11-11 Kudankita, Chiyoda-ku
Tokyo 102-0073
Japan

Tel: 03-3511-4392
Fax: 03-3511-4391

Preface

Hear Here! provides learners of English with interesting material to actively engage them in improving their listening skills. The textbook may be used by upper-beginner to intermediate learners, as implementation for different levels will depend on individual teachers, approaches, and learning situations.

Approach: The textbook contains 14 topic-based units covering a wide variety of everyday situations and encounters and employs a direct, practical approach to learning. Each unit includes activities and question types that require learners to comprehend general or specific information, such as the spelling of names, numbers and words, identifying key information, and choosing answers from given options. Moreover, the recordings include features typical of spoken English, like pauses, false starts, filler words, and clarification, etc.

Content: Each unit begins with non-listening activities to stimulate background knowledge and interest in the topic. First, two warm-up questions are presented to encourage discussion and exploration of the unit topic. Then, a topic-related vocabulary exercise follows to extend topic awareness and interest. Each unit also contains an activity that focuses on one particular phonological aspect of listening, such as weak, dropped, or linking sounds, etc. The bulk of each unit is comprised of short and longer listening passages containing mostly two-way communication, with some of the longer listening passages and activities separated into two or three parts to avoid listening overload.

English: Textbooks sometimes focus on English spoken in one particular country, which limits a learner's ability to cope with different accents and patterns of pronunciation and intonation. However, English is, of course, a global communication medium, spoken by people of different nationalities, and with this in mind, the textbook exposes learners to different accents in order to develop flexible and competent listening skills.

Plus! Hear Here! can also play a valuable role in assisting learners to attain desired results in business and academic English proficiency tests such as TOEIC, TOEFL iBT, and IELTS. Furthermore, it should not be overlooked that, while **Hear Here!** is a listening skills textbook, the language in the transcripts provides samples of spoken English that may also be studied by learners to extend their speaking ability.

Anthony Allan

Table of Contents

Unit Overview

Each unit consists of 6 pages, and directions are given below on the basic organization of unit activities. Apart from the first and second pages, activities on remaining unit pages are varied, and the general approach is as follows.

各 Unit は 6 ページ構成です。以下に Unit の構成と使い方を説明します。各 Unit の構成は、1 ページ目と 2 ページ目を除いて Unit ごとに異なりますが、基本的なアプローチは以下のようになります。

Warm-Up Questions

Each unit begins with warm-up questions to raise learner awareness about and facilitate classroom discussion on aspects relating to the unit's theme.

各 Unit で扱われているトピックに関して、質問に答えたり話し合ったりして、トピックに対する関心を高めます。

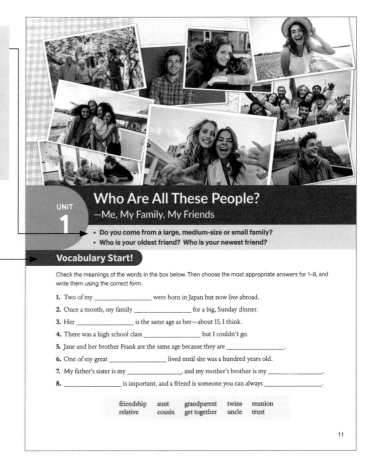

Vocabulary Start!

Learners study essential theme-related lexical items and use them to complete gap-fill sentences by selecting appropriate answers.

各 Unit に出てくる重要な語句の意味と使い方を学習します。文全体の意味を考えながら、空欄に適切な語句を選んで入れましょう。

S Conversations: Numbers and Dates

The approximate length of each recording is indicated as **S** (short), **M** (medium-length) or **L** (long) before the activity title.

アクティビティで聞く音声の長さはさまざまです。タイトルの左には、その音声の長さを示すアイコンが付いていて、短いもの（Short）は **S**、中程度のもの（Medium-length）は **M**、長いもの（Long）は **L** で表しています。

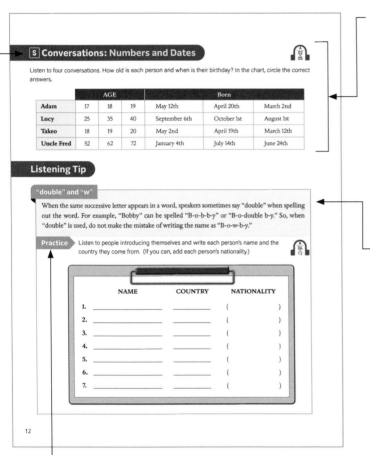

The first listening activity of each unit contains short single utterances, short exchanges, or short monologues containing a small volume of information that enables learners to ease into listening activities.

各 Unit の最初のリスニング活動は、短い単文や会話、パッセージが素材になっています。まず短いものから始めて、少しずつ長い会話やパッセージを聞くことに慣れていきましょう。

Listening Tip

This section explains a particular point of difficulty learners often encounter when listening to native English speakers.

英語のリスニングをする際に学習者が聞き取りにくいポイントを取り上げて、その特徴や聞き取りのコツなどを解説しています。

Practice

Learners focus on the **Listening Tip** point and practice it through an activity that enables familiarity with this feature of natural spoken English.

Listening Tip で取り上げたポイントを、実際にリスニングをして聞き取る練習をします。英語らしい音の特徴に慣れていくことができます。

Learners are exposed to a variety of listening situations in English, including announcements, conversations, interviews, and news reports, etc. The content language is similar to that which is typically used by English speakers in such situations, and with diverse question types, interest can be maintained and learning continued. Moreover, *Hear Here!* contains "living language," which can also facilitate practice of speaking skills in English.

アナウンス、インタビュー、ダイアログ、ニュースなどさまざまな種類や分野の英語のリスニングを行います。その内容は英語圏の国々で日常的に使われているものばかりです。設問形式もさまざまなので、飽きずに楽しくリスニングの学習を続けられます。生きた英語表現が使われているので、スピーキングに活用する練習もしてみましょう。

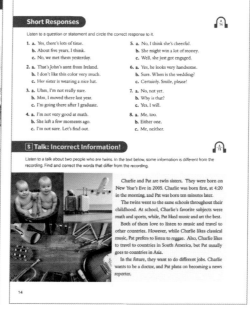

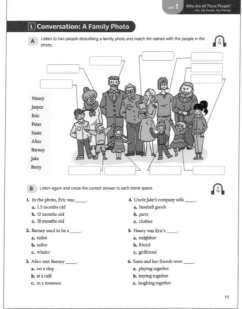

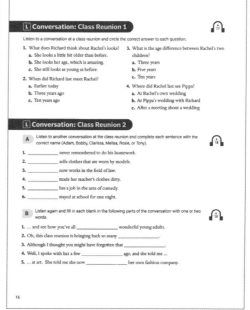

How to Access the Audio Online

For activities with a headset icon , the audio is available at the website below.

https://ngljapan.com/hrhr-audio/

You can access the audio as outline below.

❶ Visit the website above.
❷ Click the link to the content you would like to listen to.

Alternatively, scan the QR code with a smartphone or tablet to visit the website above.

音声ファイルの利用方法

 のアイコンがある箇所の音声ファイルにアクセスできます。

https://ngljapan.com/hrhr-audio/

❶ 上記の URL にアクセス、または QR コードをスマートフォンなどのリーダーでスキャン
❷ 表示されるファイル名をクリックして音声ファイルをダウンロードまたは再生

Who Are All These People?
—Me, My Family, My Friends

- **Do you come from a large, medium-size or small family?**
- **Who is your oldest friend? Who is your newest friend?**

Vocabulary Start!

Check the meanings of the words in the box below. Then choose the most appropriate answers for 1–8, and write them using the correct form.

1. Two of my _____ were born in Japan but now live abroad.

2. Once a month, my family _____ for a big, Sunday dinner.

3. Her _____ is the same age as her—about 15, I think.

4. There was a high school class _____ but I couldn't go.

5. Jane and her brother Frank are the same age because they are _____.

6. One of my great _____ lived until she was a hundred years old.

7. My father's sister is my _____, and my mother's brother is my _____.

8. _____ is important, and a friend is someone you can always _____.

friendship	aunt	grandparent	twins	reunion
relative	cousin	get together	uncle	trust

S Conversations: Numbers and Dates

Listen to four conversations. How old is each person and when is their birthday? In the chart, circle the correct answers.

	AGE			Born		
Adam	17	18	19	May 12th	April 20th	March 2nd
Lucy	25	35	40	September 6th	October 1st	August 1st
Takeo	18	19	20	May 2nd	April 19th	March 12th
Uncle Fred	52	62	72	January 4th	July 14th	June 24th

Listening Tip

"double" and "w"

When the same successive letter appears in a word, speakers sometimes say "double" when spelling out the word. For example, "Bobby" can be spelled "B-o-b-b-y" or "B-o-double b-y." So, when "double" is used, do not make the mistake of writing the name as "B-o-w-b-y."

Practice Listen to people introducing themselves and write each person's name and the country they come from. (If you can, add each person's nationality.)

	NAME	COUNTRY	NATIONALITY
1.	_____	_____	( )
2.	_____	_____	( )
3.	_____	_____	( )
4.	_____	_____	( )
5.	_____	_____	( )
6.	_____	_____	( )
7.	_____	_____	( )

S Speech: Hello, Everyone!

A Listen to a student introducing herself to her new classmates and fill in the information.

A
13

- Student's name   *Katherine* _____
- Nickname   _____
- Pets' names   _____
- Birthday   _____
- Student's age   _____
- Siblings   _____
- Their names & ages   _____
- Hometown   _____
- Date arrived   _____
- Reason   _____

B Listen again and circle T for *True* or F for *False*.

A
13

1. People often spell the student's last name incorrectly.   T   F
2. The student often argues and fights with her two siblings.   T   F
3. Her family arrived in Miami a few months ago.   T   F
4. Until now, the student had only lived in Boston.   T   F
5. The student's mother will work as the school's nurse.   T   F

C Listen again and fill in each blank with one, two, or three words.

A
13

1. I'm quite _____ but, um, I'm _____ to meet my new classmates …
2. However, the spelling is not _____ as the school's name, …
3. We _____ really well and I love them both, although sometimes …
4. … so we're still settling in and trying to _____ the warm weather here.
5. … of course the weather is much colder _____ than _____.

Short Responses

Listen to a question or statement and circle the correct response to it.

1. **a.** Yes, there's lots of time.
   b. About five years, I think.
   c. No, we met them yesterday.

2. **a.** That's John's aunt from Ireland.
   b. I don't like this color very much.
   c. Her sister is wearing a nice hat.

3. **a.** Uhm, I'm not really sure.
   b. Mm, I moved there last year.
   c. I'm going there after I graduate.

4. **a.** I'm not very good at math.
   b. She left a few moments ago.
   c. I'm not sure. Let's find out.

5. **a.** No, I think she's cheerful.
   b. She might win a lot of money.
   c. Well, she just got engaged.

6. **a.** Yes, he looks very handsome.
   b. Sure. When is the wedding?
   c. Certainly. Smile, please!

7. **a.** No, not yet.
   b. Why is that?
   c. Yes, I will.

8. **a.** Me, too.
   b. Either one.
   c. Me, neither.

S Talk: Incorrect Information!

Listen to a talk about two people who are twins. In the text below, some information is different from the recording. Find and correct the words that differ from the recording.

Charlie and Pat are twin sisters. They were born on New Year's Eve in 2005. Charlie was born first, at 4:20 in the morning, and Pat was born ten minutes later.

The twins went to the same schools throughout their childhood. At school, Charlie's favorite subjects were math and sports, while, Pat liked music and art the best.

Both of them love to listen to music and travel to other countries. However, while Charlie likes classical music, Pat prefers to listen to reggae. Also, Charlie likes to travel to countries in South America, but Pat usually goes to countries in Asia.

In the future, they want to do different jobs. Charlie wants to be a doctor, and Pat plans on becoming a news reporter.

L Conversation: A Family Photo

A Listen to two people describing a family photo and match the names with the people in the photo.

Nancy

Jasper

Eric

Peter

Susie

Alice

Barney

Jake

Betty

B Listen again and circle the correct answer to each blank space.

1. In the photo, Eric was _____.
   a. 1.5 months old
   b. 12 months old
   c. 18 months old

2. Barney used to be a _____.
   a. tailor
   b. sailor
   c. whaler

3. Alice met Barney _____.
   a. on a ship
   b. at a café
   c. in a museum

4. Uncle Jake's company sells _____.
   a. baseball goods
   b. parts
   c. clothes

5. Nancy was Eric's _____.
   a. neighbor
   b. friend
   c. girlfriend

6. Susie and her friends were _____.
   a. playing together
   b. staying together
   c. laughing together

L Conversation: Class Reunion 1

Listen to a conversation at a class reunion and circle the correct answer to each question.

1. What does Richard think about Rachel's looks?
   a. She looks a little bit older than before.
   b. She looks her age, which is amazing.
   c. She still looks as young as before.

2. When did Richard last meet Rachel?
   a. Earlier today
   b. Three years ago
   c. Ten years ago

3. What is the age difference between Rachel's two children?
   a. Three years
   b. Five years
   c. Ten years

4. Where did Rachel last see Pippa?
   a. At Rachel's own wedding
   b. At Pippa's wedding with Richard
   c. After a meeting about a wedding

L Conversation: Class Reunion 2

A Listen to another conversation at the class reunion and complete each sentence with the correct name (Adam, Bobby, Clarissa, Melisa, Rosie, or Tony).

1. _____ never remembered to do his homework.

2. _____ sells clothes that are worn by models.

3. _____ now works in the field of law.

4. _____ made her teacher's clothes dirty.

5. _____ has a job in the area of comedy.

6. _____ stayed at school for one night.

B Listen again and fill in each blank in the following parts of the conversation with one or two words.

1. … and see how you've all _____ wonderful young adults.

2. Oh, this class reunion is bringing back so many _____.

3. Although I thought you might have forgotten that _____.

4. Well, I spoke with her a few _____ ago, and she told me …

5. … at art. She told me she now _____ her own fashion company.

I'm a Bookworm
—Daily Life and Hobbies

- **How are your weekdays different from your weekends?**
- **What were your hobbies when you were a child?**

Vocabulary Start!

Check the meanings of the words in the box below. Then choose the most appropriate answers for 1–8, and write them using the correct form.

1. In my _____, I enjoy swimming and cycling.

2. My baby sister always takes a 1-hour nap around _____.

3. They usually jog but _____ they just walk.

4. You must _____ for coffee and a chat.

5. After I eat breakfast, I do the _____.

6. Are you always so _____ in the morning?

7. People in society _____ machines far too much.

8. I _____ at my local gym _____ a week.

machine	midday	free time	busy	sometimes
housework	come around	work out	once	rely on

Listen to ten people speaking about daily activities and check ☑ the correct answer to each question.

How often does he/she ...?

1. ... drink tea?	☐ Once	☐ Twice	☐ Three times	**a day**
2. ... cook?	☐ Once	☐ Twice	☐ Three times	**a day**
3. ... use public transportation?	☐ Once	☐ Twice	☐ Three times	**a day**
4. ... go shopping for food?	☐ Once	☐ Twice	☐ Three times	**a week**
5. ... go cycling?	☐ Once	☐ Twice	☐ Three times	**a week**
6. ... work P/T?	☐ Once	☐ Twice	☐ Three times	**a week**
7. ... play golf?	☐ Once	☐ Twice	☐ Three times	**a month**
8. ... visit relatives?	☐ Once	☐ Twice	☐ Three times	**a month**
9. ... travel to other countries?	☐ Once	☐ Twice	☐ Three times	**a year**
10. ... see a musical?	☐ Once	☐ Twice	☐ Three times	**a year**

Listening Tip

Numbers

Listening for numbers is an important skill. Here are three points to remember:
1. English speakers also say "**oh**" for "**zero**."
2. "**For**" often sounds like "**four**."
3. Stress in "thir**teen**" is placed on the second syllable, and in "**thir**ty" it is on the first syllable.

Practice Listen and write the numbers you hear in the sentences.

1. ☐   2. ☐   3. ☐   4. ☐   5. ☐

6. ☐ , ☐   7. ☐ , ☐   8. ☐ , ☐

S Speeches: Behavior I Don't Like!

A 28 ▾ 33

What does each speaker not like? Listen and circle the correct answer to each question.

1. She doesn't like it when people are _____ when she is at a restaurant.

a. talking **b.** smoking **c.** joking

2. He doesn't like it when people _____ loudly on trains.

a. sing **b.** play music **c.** talk

3. She doesn't like it when her boyfriend doesn't pick up _____ that are on the floor.

a. his clothes **b.** her clothes **c.** any leaves

4. He doesn't like it when people leave his apartment's _____ open, especially when the weather is bad.

a. back door **b.** windows **c.** closet doors

5. She doesn't like it when young people on bicycles wear headphones and can't hear her _____.

a. car **b.** bicycle **c.** scooter

6. He doesn't like it when people in his house leave _____ that are dirty and become smelly in the kitchen.

a. tissues **b.** clothes **c.** dishes

M Speech: My Morning Routine

Listen to a man talking about the beginning of his typical weekday and fill in the schedule.

A 34

BEGINNING of a TYPICAL WEEKDAY

... first, he __wakes up__ at around 5:30

1. ... _____ his dog for a walk

2. ... sometimes _____ a friend and chats

3. ... _____ back home at 6 o'clock

4. ... _____ the laundry _____ the washing machine ... takes a quick shower

5. ... _____ Sandy's food and water

6. ... _____ and eats breakfast

7. ... always _____ the news on the local radio station

8. ... _____ the dishes

9. ... _____ the clothes: outside or inside ... gets dressed for work

10. ... finally, _____ home around half past seven

M Speech: My Evening Routine

Listen to the man talking about the end of his typical weekday and circle T for *True* or F for *False*.

1.	He usually returns to his home at a quarter past eleven.	T	F
2.	If the laundry is outside, he takes it in before making dinner.	T	F
3.	He often eats out, but sometimes he has meals delivered.	T	F
4.	When he has dinner at home, he likes watching a particular TV program.	T	F
5.	While he is in bed, he checks his e-mail and surfs the Internet.	T	F
6.	Before going to sleep, he sets his alarm clock for half past five.	T	F

M Speech: If I Could …

Listen to a woman talking about what she usually does and fill in the information. Then listen again and fill in the information for what she would like to do.

USUAL ROUTINE

Gets up at _____ o'clock

Has a _____

Eats a _____ breakfast

Walks, rides _____ to work

Travels for _____ hour

Works as a _____ (ad company)

Works from _____ until _____

BUT WOULD LIKE TO …

Get up at _____ o'clock

Take a long, relaxing bath

Eat a _____ breakfast

_____ to work

Travel for _____ hour

Work as a _____ photographer

Work from 1 to _____ p.m.

L Interview: A Student's Survey

A Listen to a student interviewing someone and fill in each blank in the following parts of the interview with one word. The first letter of each word is given.

1. … and I'm doing a survey on l_____ h_____ .

2. Hm, well, I read an o_____ n_____ …

3. … as you can see, I'm a b_____ o_____ …

4. So I end up doing all the h_____ and l_____ , etc.

5. because we're members of an a_____ c_____ .

B Listen again and number the questions in the order the interviewer asks him.

A 37

☐ Housework—how much time do you spend doing that?

☐ How often do you play a sport or do some kind of physical exercise?

☐ How often do you read a book?

☐ How often do you meet friends for social activities?

☐ Do you listen to music a lot?

☐ How about television—do you watch much?

C Listen again and circle the correct answer to each question the interviewer asks.

A 37

Q1.	almost every day	two times a week	four times a week
Q2.	5 days a week	7 days a week	2 days a week
Q3.	sometimes	always	never
Q4.	4 hours a week	14 hours a week	40 hours a week
Q5.	1 hour a week	3 hours a week	6 hours a week
Q6.	once a week	two times a week	once every six months

S Lecture: Most Popular Hobbies

Part 1 Listen to the first part of a professor's lecture about the most popular hobbies and fill in each blank with one or two words.

A 38

1. Good morning, everyone. Today I'm going to present _____ the top ten hobbies in the world.

2. … we do hobbies based on things that we're _____, and we simply enjoy doing them.

3. Moreover, it always gives us something to look _____, especially when we feel stressed out.

4. Another reason is to create social _____ other people.

5. … but the majority involve communicating with other people and creating new _____.

6. … these factors help to keep us happy, and in many cases, _____ individuals.

Part 2 Listen to the last part of the professor's lecture and rank the popularity of the hobbies from 1st to 10th.

RANK	HOBBY	RANK	HOBBY
☐	DIY (do-it-yourself)	☐	working out
☐	arts and crafts	☐	gardening
☐	video games	☐	watching TV shows and movies
☐	reading	☐	yoga
☐	baking	☐	board games

Short Responses

Listen to each question or statement and circle the correct response to it.

1. a. Yes, I want one.
   b. No, there isn't.
   c. Actually, I play tennis.

2. a. No, I stayed at home.
   b. I have been to this shop before.
   c. Yes, I will go to the library.

3. a. It's pretty cold, isn't it?
   b. Yes, we need a new one.
   c. Then let's go shopping.

4. a. It depends on the weather.
   b. All the time.
   c. Of course, I do.

5. a. I haven't checked my e-mail, yet.
   b. Usually just after breakfast.
   c. We'll leave around 9 o'clock.

6. a. Thank you. Shall we have some tea there?
   b. You're welcome. I spent a lot of time on it.
   c. Never mind. I'll plant some new flowers.

M Speech: My Best Gadget

A Listen to someone talking about the most important item of technology they use in daily life, and fill in each blank with one or two words.

1. The speaker talks about a _____.

2. It has an _____ setting, a stopwatch, and a _____.

3. It can tell the air _____ and altitude _____.

4. It can check your _____, and it is _____.

B Listen again. How many times does the person say (repeat) the answer words in Question 1 in **A**?

_____

Spill the Beans!
—People and Characteristics

- **How would describe your looks and personality?**
- **Do you think you are more like your mother or father?**

Vocabulary Start!

Check the meanings of the words in the box below. Then choose the most appropriate answers for 1–8, and write them using the correct form.

1. Jim never does any work. He's so _____!

2. You're not short. I'd say you are _____.

3. Our company is very _____ with pay and holidays.

4. Wow, you look so _____! How much weight have you lost?

5. I'm losing my hair and am worried that I might become _____.

6. That dog is so _____! Look, it can walk on two legs.

7. I wonder why some people are _____ but others are _____.

8. Mai is a very _____ person. She _____ everyone she meets.

shy	generous	get on well with	friendly	lazy
clever	outgoing	average height	bald	slim

S Announcement: Where's Zack?

Listen to an announcement about a lost boy and write a short answer to each question.

1. What is the boy's name?

> Zack

2. How old is he?

> [ ] and a- [ ] -years old

3. How tall is he?

> ...Around [   ]

4. What is his hair like?

> ...Short, [   ]

5. What is he wearing?

> A [   ] and [   ]

6. What does he have with him?

> A brown [   ]

7. Where was he last seen?

> Near the Mega [   ] store

8. Who should customers contact?

> Someone at an [   ]

Listening Tip

Particular Word Stress

The focus of a sentence can depend on which word is particularly stressed. For example, the sentence "He lives in the city" could have four possible focuses. If "**He**" is stressed, it means "not me," etc. If "**lives**" is stressed, it means "not works," etc. If "**in**" is stressed, it means "not near," etc., and if "**city**" is stressed, it means "not the suburbs," etc.

Practice ▶ Listen to these same five statements and circle the word that receives the greatest stress in each statement.

1. Sam works in an old building near the library.

2. Sam works in an old building near the library.

3. Sam works in an old building near the library.

4. Sam works in an old building near the library.

5. Sam works in an old building near the library.

S Interviews: Who Do You Admire Most?

A Listen to a man interviewing people about which famous person they admire the most. Match each speaker with the person they admire the most.

SPEAKER	ADMIRES
Amir •	• Aung San Suu Kyi
Greta •	• Marie Curie
Stacey •	• Bill Gates
Yoon-Soo •	• Nelson Mandela
Joanna •	• Mozart

B Listen to each speaker again and circle the words that are used to describe the famous people they admire.

Bill Gates:
boring   generous
smart   calm   clever
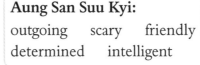

Aung San Suu Kyi:
outgoing   scary   friendly
determined   intelligent

Mozart:
serious   gifted   kind
amazing   sensitive

Nelson Mandela:
patient   strange   gentle
funny   clever

Marie Curie:
lazy   shy   caring
interesting   hard-working

Short Responses

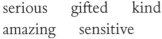

Listen to each question or statement and circle the correct response to it.

1. a. He likes reading novels.
   b. He's very talkative.
   c. He's a good teacher.

2. a. You look slim to me.
   b. You should eat a little more.
   c. I don't like exercising.

3. a. No, but he has a beard.
   b. Yes, below his mouth.
   c. Maybe he shaved his head.

4. a. Did you ask my father?
   b. Okay, I'll ask her tomorrow.
   c. She's amazing, isn't she?

5. a. It means "gentle."
   b. You can say "kind."
   c. Two words are better.

6. a. That's impossible for him.
   b. I'll repeat that for you.
   c. Sorry. What did you say?

Ⓛ Conversation: Reporting a Missing Person

Part 1   Listen to a woman calling a police station to report a missing person and circle T for *True* or F for *False*.

1. The caller's grandmother is missing.   T   F
2. The missing person is visiting the countryside for a few days.   T   F
3. The missing person's family name is Cwombes.   T   F
4. The missing person isn't carrying a mobile phone.   T   F
5. The missing person went out to buy a newspaper, bread, and jam.   T   F

Part 2   Listen as the conversation continues. One thing is incorrect in each sentence. Listen and correct it.

1. The caller's family member was wearing beige pants, a navy-blue sweater, a white shirt and a coat.
2. The family member is medium height, about 175 centimeters tall and a little underweight.
3. The family member did not appear to be sad or depressed, and is sometimes cheerful.
4. The police officer will send a patrol car to search for the family member in the morning.

Part 3   Listen to the woman calling the police station for the second time and circle the correct answer to each question.

1. When does the woman make the second call to the police station?
   a. Half an hour later
   b. One hour later
   c. Two hours later

2. Who did the grandfather meet in the corner store?
   a. Someone he used to work with.
   b. Someone who went to the same school as him.
   c. Someone who was in trouble and needed help.

3. Where did they eat lunch after leaving the store?
   a. In a bar
   b. In the park
   c. At a café

4. Where did the grandfather read his newspaper?
   a. At a café
   b. In the park
   c. In a bar

5. Why didn't the missing person call his family?
   a. He couldn't find a public phone.
   b. He didn't think it was necessary.
   c. He couldn't remember their phone number.

6. Why is the caller's grandmother angry?
   a. Because her husband didn't telephone her.
   b. Because her husband didn't buy some food.
   c. Because her husband came back after midnight.

L Conversation: First Date

A   Listen to a conversation between two friends and circle the words you hear.   🎧 A/58

expensive	mysterious	dangerous	chilly	smart	romantic	warm

beautiful	cheap	practical	generous	casual	kind	new	mean

B   Listen to the conversation again and complete each answer with two words.   🎧 A/58

GOOD THINGS

Q1. Why didn't Helen know where she and Mathew were going on their date?

A She didn't know where they were going because it was _____.

Q2. What did they do for 15 minutes?

A They took a _____ and saw the night view of the city.

Q3. Where did they eat a delicious dinner?

A They ate at a 5-star _____ on the other side of the lake.

NOT SO GOOD THINGS

Q1. How did Matthew pick her up?

A He picked her up on _____.

Q2. Where did they stop on the way to the airfield?

A They stopped at a _____.

Q3. What did Matthew expect Helen to do at the end of their meal?

A He expected her to pay _____ at the restaurant.

27

M Speeches: Perfect Love

Part 1 A Listen to part of a TV show that tries to match young couples and write each person's age, birthday, and how long they have been single for or when they last went on a date.

NAME	AGE	BIRTHDAY	STAR SIGN	SINGLE FOR?/LAST DATE?
Steve			Virgo	
Donna			Pisces	
Akira			Gemini	
Mandy			Capricorn	

Part 1 B Choose one person from the four people above. Then listen again and take notes on his/her likes and dislikes.

NAME	LIKES	DOESN'T LIKE

Part 2 Listen to the TV show's host talking about the two couples and match each person with the personality traits used to describe them.

Steve

Donna

- active •
- boring •
- honest •
- curious •
- shy •
- funny •
- hardworking •
- cheerful •
- interesting •
- outgoing •
- friendly •

Akira

Mandy

This Is Your Captain Speaking
—Vacations and Travel

- **Are there any countries you want to visit in the future? Why?**
- **Which is more enjoyable for you, traveling by land, sea or air?**

Vocabulary Start!

Check the meanings of the words in the box below. Then choose the most appropriate answers for 1–8, and write them using the correct form.

1. The _____ was delayed by an hour due to bad weather in the area.

2. It was a long _____ from our hotel to the first sightseeing spot.

3. On airplanes, I don't like window seats, so I always sit in a seat by the _____.

4. _____ are not allowed to smoke inside trains or planes.

5. I arrived safely in Sydney, but my _____ went to Perth.

6. The _____ from the top of the mountain was breathtaking.

7. First, we have to go through _____ and then _____.

8. Our plane _____ at 10 a.m. and _____ in Miami two hours later.

journey	immigration	luggage	customs	aisle
passenger	land	scenery	take off	flight

S Announcements: In the Airport

Listen to the following announcements inside an airport and fill in each blank space.

1. This is an urgent _____ for Mr. Marvin Clay. Would you please come to the Europe-One Airways check-in _____.

2. Ladies and gentlemen, may I have your attention, please. We're sorry to announce that all flights to Bangkok, _____ have been canceled due to bad _____ there.

3. This is the final boarding call for all passengers traveling to Auckland on flight _____. Please proceed to Gate _____ immediately. The flight will depart in _____ minutes.

4. Your attention, please. We are now boarding for flight _____ to London Heathrow. Would _____ class passengers please board first. Then we will ask families with _____ to board next.

5. Will passengers who arrived on flight _____ from Vancouver please pick up your _____ from carousel number _____, not carousel number _____. We apologize for any inconvenience this may cause.

Listening Tip

Sentence Word Stress

The important words (words giving concrete information) are stressed in sentences.

[Example] The underlined words are stressed in this question and response:

Q: **Kelly, how** was your **vacation**?
R: My **vacation**? Oh, it was **awesome**! I went **scuba diving**.

Practice ▶ Listen to these conversations and draw a line under the words that are stressed.

1. A: Where did you go for your vacation, Jon?
   B: I went to Bali, in Indonesia. I stayed there for three weeks.
   A: Wow, three weeks in Bali. I'm so jealous!

2. A: How was your hotel? Did you like it?
   B: Yes, it was wonderful. The ocean view was fantastic!
   A: How about the food?
   B: It was amazing, too!

M Conversation: Airport Arrival Card

Listen to two passengers talking inside an airport and fill in the arrival card.

U.S. Immigration Service	Arrival Card Welcome to the United States

Family name

First (Given) Name(s)

Sex (Gender) Male ☐ Female ☐

Nationality

Passport Number

Flight No./Vessel Name/No.

Last City/Port of Embarkation

Address in Hawaii

Length of Stay

Purpose of Stay

M Conversation: Passenger 1 Survey

Listen to the same passenger participating in a survey about his flight and circle the correct answer to each question.

1. Which airline did the passenger use?
   a. Transglobal Air
   b. Air Atlantic
   c. TransWorld Air
   d. Air Hawaii

2. Where did he start his journey?
   a. San Francisco
   b. Hawaii
   c. Boston
   d. Vancouver

3. How many minutes late did his plane depart?
   a. 0   b. 11
   c. 12   d. 20

4. Did he think the crew provided good service?
   a. Yes.
   b. No.
   c. He can't decide.
   d. It was just okay.

5. Did he enjoy the food during the flight?
   a. Yes.
   b. No.
   c. He didn't try it.
   d. It was just okay.

6. What kind of music did he listen to?
   a. Jazz   b. Hawaiian
   c. Pop   d. Rock

Listen to a different passenger participating in the survey about her flight and write a short answer to each question.

Q1. Which airline did the passenger use? **A**

Q2. Where did she start her journey? **A**

Q3. How many minutes late did her plane depart? **A**

Q4. Did she think the crew provided good service? **A**

Q5. Did she enjoy the food during the flight? **A**

Q6. What kind of music did she listen to? **A**

Short Responses

Listen to each question or statement and circle the correct response to it.

1. a. Of course. Here it is.
 b. I will buy them now.
 c. Yes, here they are.

2. a. I'm a businessperson.
 b. To visit friends.
 c. I went sightseeing.

3. a. What do you want to buy?
 b. They don't sell anything new.
 c. We already got free samples there.

4. a. I'm sorry, we don't deliver luggage.
 b. I think you should buy a new one.
 c. Please check carousel number two.

5. a. The bus stop is over there.
 b. In a few minutes, I think.
 c. The driver is not on the bus.

6. a. Yes, you can get off now.
 b. No—it's an express train.
 c. Yes, go to Platform 5.

7. a. It's a very old but beautiful building.
 b. I'm afraid I don't know.
 c. They're on the other side of town.

8. a. Okay, here we are—the zoo.
 b. Oh, I don't really like animals.
 c. Sure. It'll take about 15 minutes.

s Commercial: Vacation 1

You will hear three radio commercials for package vacations abroad. Listen to the first commercial and circle T for *True* or F for *False*.

1. This advertisement is for a vacation in Europe in fall.   T   F
2. The houses on the islands are white.   T   F
3. One healthy and popular dish is steak salad.   T   F
4. The cruise ship has three pools and five restaurants.   T   F
5. The lowest price for the cruise is $1,200.   T   F

s Commercial: Vacation 2

Listen to the second commercial and circle the correct answer for each blank space or to each question.

1. Tourists on the safari will travel in _____.
   a. an airplane   **b.** a car   **c.** a minibus

2. How many types of animals are mentioned?
   a. four   **b.** five   **c.** six

3. People on the tour will go to local _____.
   a. villages   **b.** schools   **c.** markets

4. They will learn about African _____.
   a. art   **b.** languages   **c.** customs

5. How many days is the safari?
   a. six   **b.** seven   **c.** eight

6. The cost of the trip is just _____.
   a. $1,640   **b.** $1,460   **c.** $2,640

s Commercial: Vacation 3

Listen to the third commercial and fill in each blank space in the summary.

This commercial is for a holiday in 1._____.
People on the tour will ride a 2._____ in the
desert and sleep in a 3._____ under the stars.
The tour will last for 4._____. Tourists will
be able to see the sun 5._____ and _____
over the pyramids. They can also try bargaining
for cheaper prices at local markets and enjoy
6._____ food. The cost of the trip is
7._____ per person.

33

M Announcements: Today's Flight

Listen to a pilot's announcements during a flight and complete the notes.

First Announcement

- Captain: Michael Edwards
- Golden Flight Airways
- Flight No. _____
- Flight destination: _____
- Altitude: _____ feet
- Flight time: _____ hours _____ minutes
- Present weather at destination: _____
- _____ after 1 hour
- Dinner 2 hours before plane _____
- Ask cabin crew for _____

Second Announcement

- Arriving in _____ minutes
- Fasten seatbelt, put seat forward, put away _____ in front
- Local time: _____ in the evening
- Local weather: _____, little bit _____
- Temperature: _____ Celsius
- Golden Flight Airways looks forward to serving passengers in the future
- Passengers in _____—have a smooth and _____ journey to final destination

L Speech: Walking Tour in London!

A Listen to a guide explaining a walking tour in London. Check ☑ the seven places the people will visit during the tour.

A / 79

- ☐ St. Paul's Cathedral
- ☐ London Transport Museum
- ☐ the Houses of Parliament
- ☐ River Thames cruise
- ☐ Big Ben
- ☐ Downing Street
- ☐ Westminster Abbey
- ☐ Trafalgar Square
- ☐ the London Eye
- ☐ the National Gallery
- ☐ the British Museum
- ☐ a London pub

B Listen again and write the times when the tourists will arrive at or be at the first five places.

A / 79

PLACES	Station	2nd place	3rd place	4th place	5th place
TIME					

Blow Out the Candles!
—Special Events and Holidays

- **What is one special and memorable event for you?**
- **Which national holiday do you think is the most important?**

Vocabulary Start!

Check the meanings of the words in the box below. Then choose the most appropriate answers for 1–8, and write them using the correct form.

1. I always like to _____ my birthday with my family.

2. Because tomorrow is a public holiday, will we have a _____ work?

3. It's a _____ for many people to eat turkey on Christmas Day.

4. The _____'s juggling skills were so unique and amazing!

5. My parents will celebrate their 25th wedding _____ this year.

6. Every summer, I go to the local beach to watch a _____.

7. Those _____ will hold several major _____ events next month.

8. Let's go to the international _____ and food _____ this weekend!

day off	celebrate	street performer	culture	anniversary
festival	venue	fireworks display	tradition	religious

S Speeches: Which Event?

Listen to nine recordings and write the recording number in ☐ for each event.

☐ Valentine's Day   ☐ New Year

☐ Christmas dinner   ☐ Birth of a baby

☐ Wedding ceremony   ☐ Fireworks display

☐ Spacecraft launch

☐ Birthday party

☐ College graduation ceremony

Listening Tip

Reduced Vowel Sounds

Native English speakers often replace vowel (a, e, i, o, u) sounds with the "schwa" sound, /ə/. It sounds like "uh" and is actually the most common vowel sound.

Example 1	"A": Balloon ➡ B**uh**loon	Example 2	"E": Celebrate ➡ Cel**uh**brate
Example 3	"I": President ➡ Pres**uh**dent	Example 4	"O": Freedom ➡ Freed**uh**m
Example 5	"U": Album ➡ Alb**uh**m		

Practice ▶ Following the example, listen and circle the vowel that changes, and re-write each word in 1–8 *as it sounds*, using "uh."

A
81
▼
89

Example: m a s c ⊙ t   ➡ *mascuht* _____

1. t i c k e t s   ➡ _____
2. b i r t h d a y   ➡ _____
3. c i r c u s   ➡ _____
4. t h o u s a n d   ➡ _____
5. r o c k e t   ➡ _____
6. c l a s s i c a l   ➡ _____
7. b a s k e t b a l l   ➡ _____
8. e n j o y a b l e   ➡ _____

Ⓜ Conversation: A Wedding Anniversary Gift

Part 1) **A**　Listen to a conversation and circle the correct answer for each blank space.　　A / 90

1. Eva is looking at products in a _____.
　a. store window
　b. magazine
　c. catalog

2. Soon, her parents will celebrate their _____ wedding anniversary.
　a. 5th　　　**b.** 25th　　　**c.** 55th

3. It will be a _____ wedding anniversary.
　a. ruby　　　**b.** silver　　　**c.** gold

4. Eva mentions _____ examples of gifts, such as cups, etc.
　a. four　　　**b.** five　　　**c.** six

5. To celebrate their wedding anniversary, her parents will travel to _____.
　a. Spain　　　**b.** Italy　　　**c.** Portugal

6. Previously, they went there _____.
　a. for a birthday
　b. to visit friends
　c. on their honeymoon

Part 1) **B**　Listen to the conversation again and fill in the blank space in each sentence with two words.　　A / 90

1. Actually, it's not for me. I'm _____ a gift for my parents.

2. Anyway, it's just so _____ choose something from all these gift ideas.

3. Yeah, I hate _____ gifts, too.

4. Eventually, they _____ Italy.

5. Hey, why didn't I _____ that! It's a perfect idea!

6. Ah, but this catalog doesn't _____ have any travel goods.

Part 2　Listen to the second part of the conversation and write a short answer to each question.　　A / 91

1. Apart from travel accessories, what else does the website have lots of?　_____

2. How many types of suitcases did Eva and Roger see before and after narrowing their search?　_____

3. What might be the problem with a large suitcase?　_____

4. How many suitcases and what size does the woman decide on?　_____

5. How much will she have to pay if she orders quickly?　_____

6. When will she send her order: now or tomorrow night?　_____

Short Responses

Listen to each question or statement and circle the correct response to it.

1. a. I think we can enter for free.
   b. No. It's the day after.
   c. Tomorrow is a good day.

2. a. Don't worry. You can take a boxed lunch.
   b. Don't worry. We can stand and eat there.
   c. Don't worry. It'll have lots of food stands.

3. a. Thanks! I'll be back around 11.
   b. I will. English is my favorite subject.
   c. It was great. I enjoyed it so much!

4. a. I think it was last August.
   b. Next year is my guess.
   c. It was an expensive wedding.

5. a. It wasn't noisy, was it.
   b. What time will it start?
   c. The street will be empty, right?

6. a. Yes, why not?
   b. No, I don't like your style.
   c. Maybe we should get dressed now.

7. a. I don't think so.
   b. I could take an umbrella.
   c. That would be a pity.

8. a. To forget their date of birth.
   b. To make new friends and eat cake.
   c. To celebrate becoming a year older.

M TV Report & Interview: Lift-Off!

Part 1 — Listen to a TV reporter at the launch of a space rocket and fill in the blanks.

Reporter:

Good morning! I'm reporting from the Kennedy Space Center here in Florida for a 1._____. As you can see behind me, the 2._____ NASA rocket is ready to be launched this morning. 3._____ astronauts, two from the US, one from Japan, and one from 4._____, will board the spacecraft in about an hours' time. Their 5._____ in space will last for three months and they'll conduct various 6._____ that include growing plants, 7._____, and fruit inside their spacecraft. The weather on this sunny spring today is clear with bright blue skies and the 8._____ at the moment is around 9._____ degrees Celsius, which are perfect conditions for lift-off. The local time here in Florida is 10._____ a.m. and lift-off is expected to be at noon.

Part 2 Listen to the reporter interviewing two people and circle T for *True*, F for *False*, or NG for *Not Given*.

1. The reporter thinks there are approximately eight thousand people at the event.　　T　F　**NG**

2. The couple from Japan are in Florida on their honeymoon.　　T　F　**NG**

3. It will be the first time for the couple to see the event at the actual venue.　　T　F　**NG**

4. The reporter has already seen the launch of the spacecraft twice.　　T　F　**NG**

5. The couple will travel to Walt Disney World in Orlando tomorrow.　　T　F　**NG**

6. One astronaut's lucky charm was given to him by his girlfriend.　　T　F　**NG**

Part 3 Listen to the last part of the news report and correct one word in each sentence taken from the report.

1. This is Cindy Wong reporting to you live from the Kennedy Space Station, here in Florida …

2. And with me now is the grandmother of one of the astronauts on the spacecraft.

3. I'm very excited but a little scared. I hope there are no problems with …

4. You must be very tired of your grandson, who is following in your footsteps.

5. Yes, of course. And Finland is very proud of him, too!

S Talk: Carnival Facts

Listen and write a short answer to each question about a carnival.

RIO CARNIVAL

1. What is the carnival sometimes called?
   _____

2. When does it takes place?
   _____

3. How many spectators does it attract?
   _____

4. Where are the dance school participants from?
   _____

5. What kind of decorated floats do they follow?
   _____

L Conversation: Planning a Party!

Part 1 Listen to a conversation between two friends who are planning a party and circle the correct answer for each blank space.

A 97

1. They're going to have a _____ birthday party for Wendy.
   a. surprise   b. secret   c. sudden

2. The first thing they have to decide is the _____ of the party.
   a. time   b. size   c. location

3. The party will be held on _____.
   a. Thursday, the 3rd   b. Saturday, the 23rd   c. Sunday, the 25th

4. The party will be held at a _____.
   a. community center   b. sports club   c. bowling center

5. They will take Wendy there and _____ they're going to play sports.
   a. insist   b. demand   c. pretend

6. The party will take place from _____.
   a. 5 to 7 p.m.   b. 6 to 8 p.m.   c. 7 to 9 p.m.

Part 2 Listen as the conversation continues and fill in each blank space with one word to complete three social media messages that the two friends will send about the party.

A 98

Message 1   ○ ○ ○

Hello, Eva. This is Louise. Regarding the birthday party for Wendy, would you be able to

_____ the birthday cake? Rick and I were thinking of you because we know

_____ is your _____. Please let us know.

Message 2   ○ ○ ○

Hello, everyone. Me, again. For the party, please bring a _____ _____ with

you (so, on social media, tell everyone what you'll bring). Of course, don't tell Wendy about the

party—keep it a _____!

Message 3   ○ ○ ○

Hi, Jackie. Hi, Marcus. Would you guys _____ the place where we'll have Wendy's

birthday party? You'd need to _____ up the _____, etc.

Everything Came from My Own Brain
—Education and Study

- **What is your best memory from your school life?**
- **What are the easiest and most difficult aspects of studying for you?**

Vocabulary Start!

Check the meanings of the words in the box below. Then choose the most appropriate answers for 1–8, and write them using the correct form.

1. Don't forget to _____ your application by March 31st.

2. He's a little worried because his _____ have fallen recently.

3. She is studying so hard to pass the university _____.

4. Most of my friends at school _____ the music club.

5. After I _____ college, I'm going to travel around the world for a year.

6. I wonder which university I should _____, Oxford or Cambridge?

7. Oh, no! The _____ for this _____ is today and I haven't finished it yet.

8. If I want to _____, I'll need a _____ to help pay for it.

entrance exam	graduate	study abroad	apply to	submit
assignment	belong to	deadline	scholarship	grade

Listen to a conversation between two friends and write the woman's favorite and strongest subjects.

Elementary School

Favorite subject was: _____

Strongest subject was: _____

Junior High School

Favorite subject was: _____

Strongest subject was: _____

High School

Favorite subject was: _____

Strongest subject was: _____

Listening Tip

Dropped Sounds: "t" and "d"

When a word ends with a "t" or "d" sound and the next word begins with a consonant sound, the "t" or "d" can disappear.

| Example 1 | I couldn**'t** understand the question. ➡ I couldn(-) understand the question. |
| Example 2 | I nee**d** to change the lesson time. ➡ I nee(-) to change the lesson time. |

Practice ▶ Listen to each sentence and circle the letter "t" or "d" where its sound disappears.

1. Help me, Tom. I can't understand this lecture!

2. We didn't study in the library yesterday.

3. The teacher said I need to review for the test tomorrow.

4. He told me he wouldn't hand in his essay late.

5. Where do they want to go for lunch?

6. I'm not sure. I might go, but I might not like it.

M Conversation: Tommy's Exam Results...

B
09

Listen to a conversation between a mother and son and fill in the son's missing exam scores and grades.

SUBJECT	EXAM SCORE	GRADE
Art		A+
English Literature	92	
Geography		B
History	83	
Information Technology	88	B+
Math	65	
Music		
Physical Education		A
Science	85	
Social Studies		A

Short Responses

B
10

Listen to each question and circle the correct response to it.

1. a. It was not so good.
   b. A little bit hard.
   c. They'll be easy for me.

2. a. Well, not so good.
   b. That's not bad.
   c. No, not that much.

3. a. I'd say, pretty good.
   b. It's not bad.
   c. No, I don't like them.

4. a. Yes, I guess that's true.
   b. Oh, almost every day.
   c. No, you log in here.

5. a. Yes, music is a strong subject for me.
   b. I'd definitely have to say science.
   c. I'm not very good at languages.

6. a. I handed it in this morning.
   b. I love looking at old buildings.
   c. It was signed in 1845, I think.

7. a. I'll be twenty-two, I think.
   b. Probably after three years.
   c. Something related to architecture.

8. a. I'm sorry, I don't know the time.
   b. Yes, we'll be there soon.
   c. Certainly. What is it?

L Conversation: Campus Map

Part 1 Listen to two students talking at the main entrance of a college campus and match these four buildings with the correct locations (a – j) on the map.

Library = ☐   Administration Building = ☐

Pinter Building = ☐   Morton Building = ☐

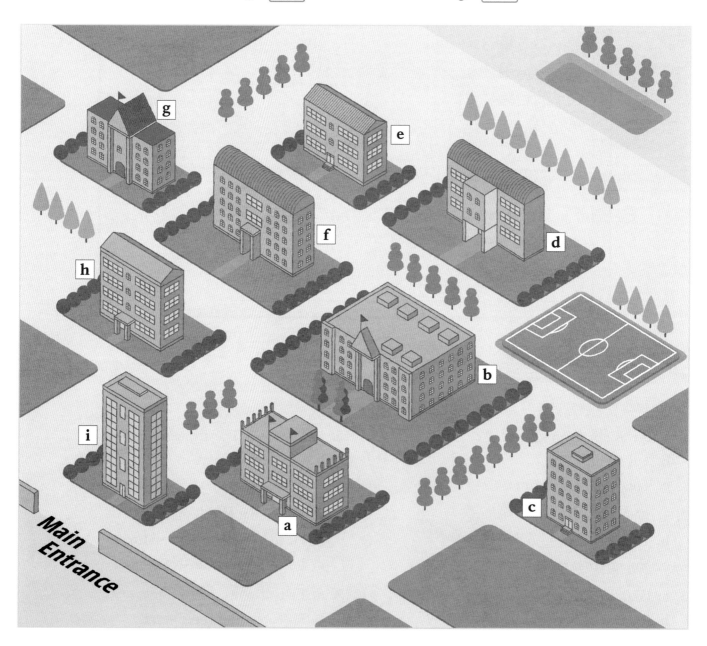

Part 2 Listen as the conversation continues and match these four buildings with the correct locations (a – j) on the map.

Albright Building = ☐   Fielding Hall = ☐   College café = ☐   Sports Center = ☐

M Conversation: A Year Abroad

Listen to a conversation between two friends and complete each short answer.

Q1. Why does Eri want to study in an English-speaking country?

A To _____.

Q2. Which country will she probably go to?

A To _____.

Q3. Why did she go there before?

A On _____.

Q4. What does the country have all year round?

A A _____.

Q5. What is the first main reason for choosing that country?

A She has _____.

Q6. What is the second main reason for choosing that country?

A Its high _____.

M Conversation: Assignment Deadline

Listen to a conversation between two students and circle T for *True*, F for *False*, or NG for *Not Given*.

1. The essay assignment must be handed in by 2:00 p.m. today.	T	F	NG
2. The length of the assignment is 2,000 words.	T	F	NG
3. James has written just under 1,000 words so far.	T	F	NG
4. Jenny used AI software to write part of her essay.	T	F	NG
5. Jenny gets ideas for her assignments from other students, family and friends.	T	F	NG
6. Jenny advises James to take notes as he talks with her.	T	F	NG

L Speech: A Guest Speaker

Part 1   Listen to a guest speaker giving a talk at a college and circle the correct answer for each blank space.

B 15

1. The speaker is _____.
   a. a current teacher
   b. a former student
   c. a current student

2. She majored in _____.
   a. economics
   b. politics
   c. business studies

3. She mostly stays in touch with friends _____.
   a. by meeting them
   b. by social media
   c. by phone

4. She is her company's _____.
   a. CEO   b. CFO   c. COO

5. Pure Packaging has offices in _____.
   a. one major country
   b. three major cities
   c. five major cities

6. The company will establish new _____ in South America and Africa.
   a. factories
   b. offices
   c. features

Part 2   Listen as the talk continues and answer the questions below.

B 16

1. Check ☑ the courses the speaker mentions.

   ☐ accounting   ☐ business ethics   ☐ international business
   ☐ commercial law   ☐ information technology   ☐ business statistics
   ☐ management and administration   ☐ domestic business   ☐ human resources
   ☐ finance   ☐ marketing   ☐ economic trends

2. What three skills does the speaker mention?

   [   ]   [   ]   [   ]

Part 3   Listen as the talk continues and circle T for *True* or F for *False*.

B 17

1. The speaker worked at a furniture store to gain practical knowledge.   T   F

2. During her internship, she learned a lot about management expectations.   T   F

3. She noticed that the company threw away many tables, cabinets, chairs, and beds.   T   F

4. She wanted to make packaging that was not bad for the environment.   T   F

5. Her company's sustainable packaging is only for furniture products.   T   F

<table>
<tr><td>UNIT
7</td><td># That Seems Reasonable
—Shopping and Money</td></tr>
</table>

That Seems Reasonable
—Shopping and Money

- **What is the best present you have ever received?**
- **What is the most expensive thing you have ever spent money on?**

Vocabulary Start!

Check the meanings of the words in the box below. Then choose the most appropriate answers for 1–8, and write them using the correct form.

1. All the _____ were very friendly and helpful, so I spent too much money!

2. I'm thinking of _____ this laptop computer or that one. I can't decide.

3. Look! There's a 70% _____ on this suit. I think I'll buy it!

4. This teapot and these cups are _____ from my holiday in England.

5. I always go shopping at BigMart because the prices are very _____.

6. Most _____ shop there in the morning, but some go in the afternoon.

7. The _____ by the station will have a winter _____ from tomorrow.

8. After paying in _____ at a vending machine, I sometimes forget to take my _____.

cash	discount	shop assistant	souvenir	change
reasonable	department store	purchase	customer	sale

Ⓢ Conversations: Which Words? The Price?

A Listen to eight short conversations and circle the words you hear in each one.

1.	dress	skirt	price tag	good bag	glad	one
2.	mug	cup	expensive	reasonable	discount	sale
3.	try	buy	looks	books	euros	yen
4.	bicycle	skateboard	models	wheels	perfect	defect
5.	clock	watch	rice	nice	budget	gadget
6.	shoes	blues	blouse	house	sale	afford
7.	sad	glad	sell	buy	cheap	reasonable
8.	advertisement	alert	silk coat	cruise ship	cleaning	dreaming

B Listen to each short conversation again and write the price each person would pay if they bought the item.

1. $_____   2. £_____   3. €_____   4. $_____

5. £_____   6. ¥_____   7. $_____   8. €_____

Listening Tip

Linking Sounds: Consonant ➡ Vowel

When a word ends with a consonant sound, the consonant sound joins the next word if the word begins with a vowel sound.

| Example | This **is** a nice shirt, Ca**n I** try **it o**n? ➡ Thi **sis** a nice shirt. Ca **ni** try **i ton**?

| Practice | Listen to each sentence and draw ‿ to show where the words link together in 1–8.

1. Just a moment, sir.

2. I'd like an apple, please.

3. Wow, look at the price!

4. Can I have a piece of cake?

5. I need a new black overcoat.

6. It's on the counter over there

7. I'm looking for a pair of socks.

8. This is all part of our service.

M Conversation: Shopping for Winter

A Listen to two people talking in a department store and circle T for *True*, F for *False* or NG for *Not Given*.

1. Karen wants to buy a pair of gloves for winter.   T   F   NG
2. Mike took Karen to the shop to buy her a scarf.   T   F   NG
3. Karen's favorite brand is not in the sale.   T   F   NG
4. Karen saw the scarf on a website today.   T   F   NG
5. It will be Karen's birthday tomorrow.   T   F   NG
6. Mike doesn't enjoy looking for birthday presents.   T   F   NG
7. There's a 30% discount on the brown leather gloves.   T   F   NG
8. Mike and Karen will pay for the presents by credit card.   T   F   NG

B Listen again and circle the correct answer for each blank space.

1. Karen probably saw the scarf _____.
   a. in a magazine
   b. on her smartphone
   c. on TV
   d. on her friend

2. On the Internet, the price of the scarf was _____.
   a. $75
   b. $85
   c. $95
   d. $105

3. Mike chose _____.
   a. black gloves
   b. sports gloves
   c. woolen gloves
   d. brown gloves

4. Karen will spend _____.
   a. $24.15
   b. $24.50
   c. $28.75
   d. $85

5. Mike will spend _____.
   a. $28
   b. $28.75
   c. $58
   d. $85

49

Short Responses

Listen to each question or statement and circle the correct response to it.

1. a. I'll take two, please.
   b. No, I don't like them, thank you.
   c. Please give me a new one.

2. a. May I try it on?
   b. Yes, I need a new suit.
   c. Do you really think so?

3. a. It's too expensive.
   b. By credit card.
   c. I accept cash.

4. a. The yellow one.
   b. Please take two.
   c. I'd like to go shopping.

5. a. Well done!
   b. That's a pity!
   c. I'm glad to hear that!

6. a. Yes, it is cheap, isn't it?
   b. Shall I wrap it for you?
   c. How about 15% off?

7. a. Okay. I'll take it with me now.
   b. Yes, we accept deliveries every day.
   c. Good. Can you tell me when?

8. a. No, because it's over a year old.
   b. No, it's still working.
   c. No, you need to bring it here.

[S] Conversations: Items, Prices & Decisions!

Listen to four conversations about shopping and complete the chart. What is each item? How much is it? Does the person buy it ☑ ?

	ITEM	PRICE	YES (√)	NO (√)
1.		£	☐	☐
2.		$	☐	☐
3.		€	☐	☐
4.		¥	☐	☐

S Speeches: Auction Time!

Part 1 Listen to an auction and fill in the details for ITEM 1 in the chart.

Part 2 Listen to an auction and fill in the details for ITEM 2 in the chart.

ITEM 1		ITEM 2	
No.		**No.**	
Item	Japanese	**Item**	European
Year	around	**Year**	roughly
Shows	images from the	**Shows**	people enjoying a ___ in a house
Condition		**Condition**	
Size	___ cm × ___ cm	**Size**	___ cm × ___ cm
Starting price	$	**Starting price**	$
Sold to	man in	**Sold to**	lady in
Sold for	$	**Sold for**	$

M Conversation: Genuine or Fake?

Listen to a conversation about shopping at a café and circle T for *True*, F for *False* or NG for *Not Given*.

1. Suzie arrived at the café first.   T   F   NG
2. Liz delivered something to someone's home.   T   F   NG
3. The bag was designed in Italy.   T   F   NG
4. Suzie's designer handbag cost her $460.   T   F   NG
5. Suzie thinks Liz's handbag is not genuine.   T   F   NG
6. Bravda only sell their products on the Internet.   T   F   NG

L Conversation: Barter, Barter!

Part 1 A Listen to a conversation at a street market in Southeast Asia and circle the correct answer to each question. 🎧 B/36

1. What kind of goods does the stall sell?
   a. T-shirts, sandals, and sun hats
   b. T-shirts, sarongs, and towels
   c. Shorts, sandals, and towels

2. Where is the tourist from?
   a. New Caledonia
   b. New Jersey
   c. New Zealand

3. How long is he on vacation?
   a. One week
   b. Two weeks
   c. Four weeks

4. How old are the tourist's nephew and niece now?
   a. 12 and 15
   b. 12 and 16
   c. 12 and 18

5. What are the colors of the rainbow on?
   a. T-shirts
   b. Towels
   c. American dollars

6. How many things does the tourist buy?
   a. Three
   b. Five
   c. Six

Part 1 B Listen again and calculate how much the tourist will pay for all of his goods. Then write the figure in the box below. 🎧 B/36

He will pay a total of $ ☐ .

Part 2 Listen to parts of the conversation and fill in the blank spaces. The number of words is indicated. 🎧 B/37

1. 2 words

   W: Hello, please _____ to look around. We have T-shirts, sarongs, and towels. They're all made locally.

2. 3 words

   M: That's pretty expensive. I'm sorry, but no thanks.
   W: _____! I'll give you a special price—two for $25. How's that?

3. 4 words

   M: And if I buy more than one?
   W: Wow! You _____! You can have them for $10 each.

4. 5 words

   M: Wow! Thank you. _____! Um, this one, please.

52

Home Sweet Home
—Accommodations and Homes

- Is it better to live in the city or the countryside? Why?
- What would be your dream home? Describe it.

Vocabulary Start!

Check the meanings of the words in the box below. Then choose the most appropriate answers for 1–8, and write them using the correct form.

1. I wonder if this hotel has any _____ for tonight?

2. He's going to _____ to Ireland to be closer to his relatives.

3. Helen _____ a large countryside mansion from her parents.

4. Remember that you must pay your _____ by the 28th of every month.

5. The _____ can take our furniture etc. to the new house on Thursday.

6. Gas! Electricity! Water! _____ charges are so high nowadays!

7. I'll call the _____ and ask if we can see the _____ tomorrow.

8. The _____ is quite old and prefers to have _____ who are quiet.

rent	inherit	landlord	move	property
vacancy	tenant	moving company	utilities	real estate agent

Listen to a woman talking about her decision regarding her home and fill in the blanks.

I like where I live but I've decided to 1._____ to a different part of the city. I want to live in a different place because my 2._____ is too far from my university and it takes over an hour to get there. Last week, I searched for a suitable 3._____ and found one that is quite convenient. Also, I met the 4._____, who seemed very nice. The monthly 5._____ is reasonable, so tomorrow I'll sign the 6._____ and then search for a 7._____ to take my things to my new home. I hope the other 8._____ in the building are nice.

Listening Tip

Repetition and Confirmation

People often repeat a key point they hear from a speaker. Then the speaker confirms the repetition.

Example | **A:** My new house has **six bedrooms**.
B: Six bedrooms?
A: Yes, and ....

Practice ▷ Listen to two conversations and fill in the blanks with the key points.

A: I just inherited _____ from a relative!

B: _____?

A: Yes. I'm rich!

A: Where do you live, Judy?

B: Actually, I have homes in _____ and _____.

A: _____ and _____!

B: That's right.

M Speech: My Dream Home!

Listen to a man describing his dream home and circle the correct answer for each blank space.

1. His dream home would be located in _____.

 a. the city center

 b. the suburbs

 c. the countryside

2. The dream home would be _____.

 a. an old castle

 b. an old church

 c. an old villa

3. The home would have six _____.

 a. bathrooms

 b. bedrooms

 c. floors

4. The swimming pool would be _____.

 a. inside the building

 b. under the building

 c. outside the building

5. There would be a _____.

 a. work out room

 b. playroom

 c. game room

6. He would travel to and from his dream house by _____.

 a. helicopter **b.** jet plane **c.** limousine

L Conversation: Cheap Accommodations . . .

Listen to two backpackers in Thailand discussing where to stay and fill in the charts. Then answer the question below the charts.

Which One?

Phuket Sunrise

(_____ baht per night)

PROS

• By beach

• Provides _____

• Has exotic _____

• Breakfast: free _____ & _____

CONS

• _____ air-conditioning

• Wi-fi connection is _____

Happy Traveler Hostel

(_____ baht per night)

PROS

• Has air-conditioning

• Near famous _____

• Free _____

• Near shops & restaurants

CONS

• Noisy _____ at night

• No _____

Q. Which accommodation will they go to, Phuket Sunrise or Happy Traveler Hostel?

L Interview: An Author's Homes

Part 1 Listen to the first part of a show and complete the notes. The show's guest is talking about places where she has lived during her life.

KEY QUESTIONS	NOTES
• Who is the guest?	• Millicent Walker: author of books on_____ and _____
• Where did she live?	• in _____ countryside
• Type of home?	• beautiful old house (small _____ nearby)
• How long lived there?	• for last _____
• Building was surrounded by?	• vineyards
• Building's age?	• _____ old
• How many floors?	• _____
• How many bedrooms?	• _____
• Favorite place in house?	• _____
• Why favorite place in house?	• _____ to _____ there

Part 2 Listen as the interview with the author continues and circle T for *True* or F for *False*.

1. The author used to live on the 15th floor of an apartment building in Central Park.   T   F

2. She didn't care about the size of her kitchen because she often ate at restaurants.   T   F

3. Every morning, she enjoyed swimming in a pool in the local park.   T   F

4. Earlier this year, she bought a house in Christchurch and is now living there.   T   F

5. The sea is close to where she is living at the moment.   T   F

6. Her new book is called *Vegetable Breakfasts,* and people will be able to buy it next month.   T   F

Short Responses

Listen to each question or statement and circle the correct response to it.

1. **a.** Yeah, I agree with you.
   b. Can we afford that?
   c. I paid it yesterday.

2. **a.** Sure. I don't see why not.
   b. Actually, it's for six months.
   c. In fact, they don't like it.

3. **a.** I can't move in this evening.

    b. Well, there's one room left.

    c. They're building them today.

4. **a.** No, it isn't.

    b. Yes, there are.

    c. I'm not sure.

5. **a.** Why are we moving again?

    b. Let's wait until we sign the contract.

    c. It's wrong to move to the city.

6. **a.** Yes. I'll go and get the keys.

    b. Of course I'm doing it properly.

    c. You might be there tomorrow.

L Conversation: Any Vacancies?

Listen to a woman calling a hotel in search of accommodations and circle T for *True*, F for *False* or NG for *Not Given*.

1. The woman is calling the Palm Garden Hotel.	T	F	NG
2. The hotel's website says there are a few vacancies.	T	F	NG
3. A group of elderly people had canceled their reservation.	T	F	NG
4. The hotel staff mentions three types of rooms.	T	F	NG
5. You can see the ocean from the upper floors of the hotel.	T	F	NG
6. Only the Luxury rooms have a refrigerator.	T	F	NG
7. The cost of a Luxury room for one night is $85.	T	F	NG
8. The woman will take a bus to get to the hotel.	T	F	NG

L Conversation: Check-In!

Listen to the woman checking in to the hotel and circle the correct answer to each question.

1. What is the hotel guest's home address?

    a. 251 Parkway Street

    b. 351 Darkway Avenue

    c. 351 Parkway Avenue

2. What is the date she checks in to the hotel?

    a. 9th August

    b. 12th August

    c. 15th August

3. What is her room number?

    a. 97   **b.** 947

    c. 907   **d.** 917

4. On which floor is the StarSky Bar?

    a. 10th   **b.** 12th

    c. 20th   **d.** 22nd

5. What can hotel guests do on the basement floor?

    a. Work out and relax

    b. Listen to live music

    c. Drink and eat

6. What is the check-out time for the guest?

    a. At noon   **b.** 10 a.m.

    c. 2 p.m.   **d.** 1 p.m.

L Conversation: ACE Real Estate

Part 1 Listen to a conversation at a real estate agency and number the questions (1–9) in the order you hear them.

☐ B/48

☐ Anything else?

☐ Please have a seat, Mr. … ?

☐ Did you have a specific location in mind?

☐ Well, I'd really like to find a nice place quickly so shall we go?

☐ How may I help you, sir?

☐ And when would you like to move in?

☐ First, what price range were you thinking of, Mr. Hart?

☐ Would I be able to see them now? Is that possible?

☐ Are there any other amenities that you'd like to have?

Part 2 Listen as the conversation continues and circle the apartment location Mr. Hart chooses. Then write notes about its good points and issues.

☐ B/49

Bridge Street

Riverside Avenue

GOOD POINTS

· _____

· _____

· _____

ISSUES

· _____

· _____

· _____

· _____

UNIT

9

I Bet You Have a Sweet Tooth
—Restaurants and Food

- **Which do you prefer, eating indoors or outdoors?**
- **What is the strangest type of food you have ever eaten?**

Vocabulary Start !

Check the meanings of the words in the box below. Then choose the most appropriate answers for 1–8, and write them using the correct form.

1. This _____ has everything: salad, soups, spaghetti, curry, bread, desserts …

2. Waiter, could we have another two _____, please?

3. Wow! You have such a large _____—you ate everything!

4. What shall we have as our _____, soup or salad?

5. Hello. I called earlier and _____ a table for three for this evening.

6. I don't eat meat, so I hope the restaurant has _____ dishes.

7. We want to _____ some fried rice _____, please.

8. She _____ seafood, so please don't use any _____ that contain fish oil.

starter	to go	ingredients	order	vegetarian
menu	appetite	book/reserve	be allergic to	buffet

S Commercials: Food, Food, Food!

Listen to three commercials and fill in the blank spaces to complete the scripts.

Commercial 1

When was the last time you ate _____ sushi? Come on down to Fuji Sushi, where you can enjoy the _____ of Japan without having to go there!

Commercial 2

Do you where you can order the best take-out pizzas? It's at Pizza _____ , of course! We have over 30 different types of _____ to suit all tastes.

Commercial 3

The number one Chinese restaurant is just around the corner no matter which _____ you live in! Eat in or take out from The Orient Express. For home deliveries, we can deliver to your _____ in 30 minutes!

Listening Tip

Mixed Sounds: "d" + "y" ➡ "dj"

When a word ends in "d" and the next word begins with "y," they join to make the sound "dj."

Example What woul**d y**ou like to order? ➡ What wou **dj**ou like to order?

Practice ▸ Listen to the questions and write in the missing words.

1. When _____ dinner party finish?

2. Why _____ friend say such a thing about your cooking?

3. Sarah, have you _____ something to drink?

4. _____ want the set meal, sir?

5. Where _____ like to sit, ma'am?

M Conversation: Samurai Sushi

B
58

Listen to a conversation and circle the items the customer orders. Then answer the question below.

Samurai Sushi

Nigiri Sushi

• Crab	¥480		• Sea eel	¥330
• Egg	¥165		• Sea urchin	¥460
• Fatty tuna	¥440		• Shrimp	¥220
• Octopus	¥175		• Squid	¥330
• Salmon	¥220		• Sweet shrimp	¥380
• Sea bream	¥185		• Tuna	¥230

Rolled Sushi

• Cucumber roll	¥275
• Eel and cucumber roll	¥580
• Fatty tuna roll	¥620
• Natto roll	¥275
• Tuna roll	¥440

All prices shown include sales tax.

Question: What is the total cost of the customer's order? ⬚

M Speeches: The Ingredients Are ...?

Part 1　Listen to a chef explaining how to make a desert and check ☑ the ingredients the chef mentions. Then answer the question.

B
59

☐ eggs
☐ milk
☐ flour
☐ white sugar
☐ whipped cream

☐ brown sugar
☐ almonds
☐ cocoa powder
☐ salt
☐ butter

Question: What is the desert?
⬚

Part 2　Listen to a chef explaining how to make a light meal and check ☑ the ingredients the chef mentions. Then answer the question.

B
60

☐ unsalted butter
☐ mushrooms
☐ corn
☐ eggs
☐ green pepper

☐ onions
☐ black pepper
☐ potatoes
☐ red pepper
☐ salt

Question: What is the light meal?
⬚

S Speeches: Chef Mistakes!

Listen to chefs explaining how to make some dishes and drinks and find one incorrect ingredient in each explanation.

- **A vegetarian salad:** The wrong ingredient is _____.
- **A cold drink:** The wrong ingredient is _____.
- **A steak sandwich:** The wrong ingredient is _____.
- **A hot drink:** The wrong ingredient is _____.

Short Responses

Listen to each statement or question and circle the correct response to it.

1. a. Do you have the menu?
    b. I'll cook in the morning.
    c. I'd rather stay in and eat.

2. a. Then send it back.
    b. I'll eat it for you.
    c. The service is slow here.

3. a. How much do they have?
    b. This milk is not fresh.
    c. Because we've run out.

4. a. Yes, I'm very thirsty.
    b. I'm full, actually.
    c. No, let's wash these dishes.

5. a. Let me taste a little first.
    b. How much time did it take?
    c. Yes, let's add some more.

6. a. Yes, I already gave it to you.
    b. Of course, you have it.
    c. I'll just get it for you.

M Conversation: Strange Snacks ...

A   Listen to a conversation and check ☑ the snack food that is eaten in each country.

	grasshoppers	frog legs	shark meat	tarantula spiders	baby ants
Cambodia	☐	☐	☐	☐	☐
France	☐	☐	☐	☐	☐
Iceland	☐	☐	☐	☐	☐
Mexico	☐	☐	☐	☐	☐
Thailand	☐	☐	☐	☐	☐

B Listen again and circle T for *True* or F for *False*.

1. Kaseem said that grasshoppers are quite soft.　　　　　　　　　T　　F

2. Astrid thought that frog legs tasted a little bit like pork.　　　　T　　F

3. Astrid said that shark meat cubes have a terrible smell.　　　　T　　F

4. The spiders Kaseem ate were fried in garlic.　　　　　　　　　T　　F

5. Astrid thinks wasabi ice cream is worse than insect snacks.　　T　　F

M Radio Program: Restaurant Reviews!

A Listen to a radio program host talking about some local restaurants. Write the country that each restaurant serves food from.

RESTAURANT	COUNTRY
• Hudson Bay	_____
• Athena	_____
• Lotus Palace	_____
• The Olive Grove	_____
• Ariba, Ariba!	_____

B Listen again and answer Questions 1–5.

Which restaurant would be best if you wanted to:

1. eat hot food surrounded by bright colors?　　_____

2. join in and enjoy a performance?　　_____

3. chat in a peaceful environment?　　_____

4. see the scenery of the local area?　　_____

5. go on a first date with someone special?　　_____

63

L Conversation: A Special Dinner

Part 1 Listen to a conversation and circle the correct answer to each question.

[B 68]

1. How many people does the woman want to make a reservation for?
   a. Two   b. Four
   c. Six   d. Twelve

2. What will the people celebrate at the dinner?
   a. An engagement   b. A birthday
   c. A wedding   d. An anniversary

3. What event will take place in town on Sunday the 19th?
   a. A fair   b. A festival
   c. A concert   d. A parade

4. When will the woman book the dinner for?
   a. Sunday, the 8th   b. Sunday, the 18th
   c. Saturday the, 17th   d. Saturday, the 18th

5. How many tables will the woman's group use at the restaurant?
   a. One   b. Two
   c. Three   d. Six

6. How many dishes will each person eat at the restaurant?
   a. One   b. Two
   c. Three   d. Four

Part 2 Listen as the conversation continues and complete the caller's notes.

[B 69]

CALLER'S NOTES

- Cost of meal: _____ per person
- Choose tea/coffee. One alcoholic beverage _____ in price.
- Meal has _____ options.
- Have to pay a deposit of _____ to reserve tables.
- Website: _____
- Deposit total: _____
- Must cancel _____ before, or lose deposit.

Part 3 Listen as the conversation continues and complete the restaurant staff's notes.

[B 70]

RESTAURANT STAFF NOTES

- Customer will bring _____ to restaurant.
- Staff to present it to _____ at end of meal.
- Keep it cool in large _____ .
- Customer will bring it at _____ .
- Customer's name: _____
- Cell phone: _____

My Ears Are Ringing!
—Going Out and Entertainment

- **How often do you go out? Who do you usually go out with?**
- **What is your favorite type of entertainment? Why?**

Vocabulary Start!

Check the meanings of the words in the box below. Then choose the most appropriate answers for 1–8, and write them using the correct form.

1. I love music, but I haven't been to a _____ for ages.

2. _____ are very popular, especially in the United States.

3. My dream is to _____ with my favorite singer.

4. This _____ has the longest ride in the world!

5. The famous _____ bought a luxury apartment in Singapore.

6. Have you ever seen any of Shakespeare's _____?

7. The _____ was so popular that it won many _____.

8. The comedy made the _____ in the _____ laugh a lot.

movie theater	concert	go on a date	audience	talk show
actor	foreign film	amusement park	play	award

S Speeches: Where Did They Go?

Listen to people talking about eight places or events and number the places in the order you hear them.

☐ Amusement park

☐ Theater play

☐ Restaurant

☐ Ice skating event

☐ Magic show

☐ Rock concert

☐ Movie theater

☐ Museum

Listening Tip

Mixed Sounds: "t" + "y" ➡ "tch"

When a word ends in "t" and the next word begins with "y," they join to make the sound "tch."

| Example | Have you decided wha**t y**ou want to see?
➡ Have you decided wha **tch**ou want to see?

Practice ▷ Listen to the questions/statements and write in the missing words.

1. Is it true _____ parents are singers?

2. _____ go with me to the museum tomorrow?

3. You went to the amusement park _____ didn't ride anything!

4. Have you decided _____ want to do this weekend?

5. Everyone thinks _____ are really good at dancing.

6. Amy, _____ go to the movies last weekend, too?

L TV Show: Master Quiz!

A Listen to a TV quiz program and circle the correct answer to each question.

1. How tall is the Eiffel Tower?
   a. 313 m
   b. 330 m
   c. 333 m
   d. 343 m

2. How tall is Tokyo Tower?
   a. 330 m
   b. 333 m
   c. 340 m
   d. 343 m

3. In which country is the world's longest road tunnel?
   a. Switzerland
   b. China
   c. Norway
   d. Japan

4. When was construction of the Sydney Opera House completed?
   a. 1959
   b. 1969
   c. 1972
   d. 1973

5. Which is the deepest ocean in the world?
   a. Pacific
   b. Indian
   c. Atlantic
   d. Arctic

6. In what year did the first human travel into space?
   a. 1941
   b. 1951
   c. 1961
   d. 1971

7. What are the largest and the second largest continents in the world?
   a. Asia, Australia
   b. Asia, Africa
   c. North America, Africa
   d. Europe, Asia

8. How long is the Nile River?
   a. 6,660 km
   b. 6,960 km
   c. 6,690 km
   d. 6,790 km

9. In what year was the World Wide Web invented?
   a. 1969
   b. 1975
   c. 1979
   d. 1989

B Listen again and add up the points to find out the winner of the quiz program.

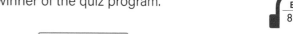

• **Molly** = [＿＿＿＿] points   • **Martin** = [＿＿＿＿] points

Short Responses

Listen to each statement or question and circle the correct response to it.

1. a. I'll go out with you.
   b. I'm fine with that.
   c. We shouldn't stay there.

2. a No, the stadium is full.
   b. No, not at the moment.
   c. No, I don't want to play.

3. a. How did you do that?
   b. How was it done?
   c. Which one?

4. a. I think they're all sold out.
   b. I'm glad we saw that show.
   c. You can only sit on the right.

5. a. Really? I'm enjoying it, too.
   b. Shall we go to the movies?
   c. Actually, I've already seen it.

6. a. Yes, it's difficult to get in there.
   b. No, my friends and I don't like it.
   c. Yes, it needs more customers soon.

7. a. I heard it's not worth going.
   b. There's a storm coming tonight.
   c. Unfortunately, the tickets are so expensive.

8. a. Yeah, let's try a different attraction.
   b. Well, a taxi would be much quicker.
   c. Okay, here we go! Hold on!

S Recording: TicketMate Tickets

Listen to a recording from a ticket service and write the correct numbers in the table.

TICKET TYPE	PRESS #	THEN #
A modern dance performance		
A local athletics event		
A drama at a theater		
A Formula 2 car race		
A musical		

L Conversation: A Scary Movie

Part 1 Listen to a conversation between a father and daughter and circle the correct answer for each blank space.

B 88

1. Terry is the name of the girl's _____.
   a. friend
   b. father
   c. boyfriend

2. The theater was showing ____ movies.
   a. three
   b. four
   c. five

3. Terry wanted to watch the _____.
   a. human drama
   b. horror movie
   c. comedy

4. Fay wanted to see the _____.
   a. human drama
   b. adventure movie
   c. comedy

5. At the movie theater, they sat together and watched the _____.
   a. adventure movie
   b. horror movie
   c. human drama

6. Fay felt _____ during the movie.
   a frightened
   b. relaxed
   c. hungry

Part 2 Listen as the conversation continues and circle T for *True* or F for *False*, or NG for *Not Given*.

B 89

1. The couple shared a big box of popcorn and a cold drink.	T	F	NG
2. Without the student discount, each ticket would have cost $12.	T	F	NG
3. All seats in the movie theater were occupied.	T	F	NG
4. The couple cleaned up the mess immediately after it happened.	T	F	NG
5. The girl bought new clothes to go on the date to the movie theater.	T	F	NG
6. The girl thinks she might see a ghost when she goes to sleep tonight.	T	F	NG

Part 3 Listen several times to part of the previous conversation and fill in each blank space with three words.

B 90

W: Well, 10 minutes into the movie a ghost suddenly appeared and both Terry and I jumped out of our seats.

M: _____—and the drinks and popcorn went everywhere.

W: Yep, _____!

M: Oh, what _____ money!

W: You can _____! But …

L TV Show: 5 Hottest Spots!

A Listen to a TV show recommending five places to go and fill in the information in the table.

VENUE	INFO.	OPENS/CLOSES	TICKETS
Central City Zoo	One of the [　　　　] zoos in the country.	Weekdays: 9:15 a.m. to [　　　　] p.m. Weekends: 8:30 a.m. to [　　　　] p.m.	One-day pass: $ [　　　]
Palace Theater	The Great Majesto performs [　　　　　　　　].	Nightly (except Tuesdays and [　　　　]) 7 to 9 p.m.	Front row seats: $65 Back, side seats: $ [　　]
The Art Colosseum	Oil paintings, sculptures, pottery and photography by famous [　　　　] and [　　　　] artists.	Every day: [　　]:00 a.m. to [　　]:00 p.m.	Adults: $40 Children, seniors, disabled: $ [　　]
Wondertime World	Exciting [　　　　] that will immediately increase your [　　　　] rate!	[　　　　] a.m. to 9:00 p.m.	One day: $85 Half day: $ [　　] (to 2 p.m.)
Seaview Aquarium	Offers great [　　　　] for [　　　　].	9:00 a.m. to [　　　　] p.m. daily (except [　　　　　　])	Adults: $30 Children: $ [　　] 2nd, 3rd child: [　　　]

B Listen again and circle T for *True* or F for *False*.

1. If you book a one-day pass before going to Central City Zoo, you can get a discount of 35%.　T　F
2. At the Palace Theater, you can see one of the nation's top, young Magicians.　T　F
3. The host thinks that the art museum's café is a good choice for eating lunch.　T　F
4. At Wondertime World, it is prohibited to take photos with some of the characters.　T　F
5. You are allowed to swim with some of the sea animals at Seaview Aquarium.　T　F

70

UNIT 11

She Sounds Promising
—Employment and Business

- **What do you worry about most in job interviews?**
- **What is an ideal work-life balance for you?**

Vocabulary Start!

Check the meanings of the words in the box below. Then choose the most appropriate answers for 1–8, and write them using the correct form.

1. The _____ is going to close, so 2,000 workers will lose their jobs.

2. Congratulations, Hana! I heard that you're going to _____ to manager.

3. My _____ and I really get along well with each other.

4. Next spring, I'm going to _____ to my company's office in Hong Kong.

5. My Uncle Harry works in _____ and builds bridges!

6. The _____ rate is very low—I think it's only 2% at the moment.

7. He'll change his _____ because he doesn't like _____ every night.

8. I signed the _____ because the company offers an excellent _____.

contract	unemployment	be transferred	construction	factory
coworker	do overtime	work environment	get promoted	occupation

71

S Speeches: What's My Occupation?

Listen to people talking about their jobs and number the jobs (1–10) in the order you hear them.

[ ] dentist

[ ] taxi driver

[ ] architect

[ ] veterinarian

[ ] tour guide

[ ] lawyer

[ ] farmer

[ ] astronaut

[ ] detective

[ ] pilot

Listening Tip

Casual English: gonna, gotta, hafta, hasta

When speakers use casual English, words and expressions are often reduced.

| Example | "going to" becomes "gonna," "got to" becomes "gotta," "have to" becomes "hafta," and "has to" becomes "hasta." |

Practice Listen to the questions/statements and circle the words that are spoken in casual English with *gonna*, *gotta*, *hafta*, or *hasta*.

1. Is everyone going to go to the job fair this weekend?

2. I've got to find a job before I graduate college.

3. He has to buy a new suit for the interviews.

4. We're going to receive a 5% pay raise in spring.

5. Do you have to start work early tomorrow?

6. She has to write a sales report, and she's got to do it soon.

M Talk: When Looking for a Job ...

Listen to someone explaining the process of searching for a job and fill in the blanks with the correct word. The first letter of each word is given.

When looking for a job, you should send your 1. r_____ to different companies. If an 2. e_____ is interested in you, they will contact you and offer you an 3. i_____. If you attend it, you'll have to answer questions about your background, skills and experience. You'll also learn details about the 4. p_____, for example, what kind of work you'll do, the working hours, and how much you'll 5. e_____, or the monthly 6. s_____. If the company wants you to become their 7. e_____, you'll receive a 8. j_____ o_____. If you accept it, and work hard, after a while you could get 9. p_____ to a better job, so your 10. i_____ will go up.

Short Responses

Listen to each question or statement and circle the correct response to it.

1. **a.** Are you looking for work?
   b. Then please fill out this form.
   c. I don't have a pen or paper.

2. **a.** On the top floor.
   b. Above this building.
   c. Under the floor.

3. **a.** I'll get a new suit tomorrow.
   b. It looks very stylish and cool.
   c. OK. I'll dress more casually from now on.

4. **a.** Yes, I think he'll get promoted soon.
   b. She should work on weekends.
   c. Well, sales are low this month.

5. **a.** No, it wasn't done.
   b. I certainly hope so.
   c. It's almost 5 o'clock.

6. **a.** Oh, I'm sorry to hear that.
   b. Oh, that's wonderful!
   c. Oh, how interesting!

Listen to two people discussing the resume of a job applicant and complete the blank spaces in the resume.

Karen Murti (Ms)

Apt. 301, 296 South _____,
Vancouver, BC, Canada T2G OW7
Tel: (502) 888-321   E-mail: aisham@arc.cot

OBJECTIVE: To obtain a position with an outdoor _____ company

RELATED SKILLS

- Red Cross First Aid and CPR _____
- Certified kayak _____
- Experienced mountain climber

PERSONAL ATTRIBUTES

- Excellent communication skills
- _____ and responsible
- Prefer working _____

EDUCATION

- Bachelor of Arts in Economics   Southport College, Vancouver, BC. 2018–_____

EMPLOYMENT

- _____   Moonrise Hotel, Calgary, Alberta Oct. 2023–Present
- Warehouse _____   Direct Deliveries, Montreal, Quebec Aug. 2022–Sep. 2023

ADDITIONAL INFORMATION

- Enjoy sports and exercise
- _____ community work
- Fluent in _____

REFERENCES

- References and _____ of recommendation available upon request

M Speeches: I Love My Job but …

Two people will talk about the pros and cons of their jobs.

Part 1 Listen to the first person, **a flight attendant**, and complete the notes below.

PROS

- Visits many _____ _____
- Stays in _____ _____
- Gets _____ _____ on airplanes
- Gets _____ _____ with own company

CONS

- Doesn't have a good _____ _____
- Is always _____
- Some passengers are very _____ —causes her _____

Part 2 Listen to the second person, **an actor**, and circle the correct answer for each blank space.

PROS

1. He gets paid well for _____.
  a. TV shows
  b. theater plays
  c. TV dramas

2. From his fans, he receives _____.
  a. letters
  b. proposals
  c. money

3. When he wins a major _____.
  a. reward
  b. hoard
  c. award

4. He gets chances to work _____.
  a. in expensive productions
  b. in other countries
  c. with international stars

CONS

1. He doesn't get paid much for _____.
  a. plays
  b. delays
  c. replays

2. His work is often _____.
  a. short
  b. unstable
  c. boring

3. His acting sometimes receives bad _____.
  a. news
  b. refuse
  c. reviews

4. Because of fans, it's difficult to have a private _____.
  a. life
  b. party
  c. audience

Ⓜ Conversation: The Perfect Job ...

Listen to a conversation at an employment agency and circle T for *True* or F for *False*.

1.	Kenny finished his education about half a year ago.	T	F
2.	He traveled to five continents after college.	T	F
3.	He made videos when he visited different places on his travels.	T	F
4.	He can communicate in French, Danish, and Italian.	T	F
5.	He doesn't want to just be at a desk when he works.	T	F
6.	The agency staff is not sure if she has a suitable position for Kenny.	T	F

Ⓛ Conversation: An Overseas Business Trip

A   Listen to a conversation about a business trip and match each person with their company.

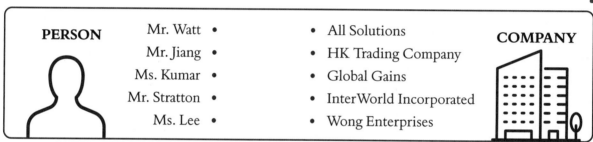

PERSON

Mr. Watt •

Mr. Jiang •

Ms. Kumar •

Mr. Stratton •

Ms. Lee •

• All Solutions

• HK Trading Company

• Global Gains

• InterWorld Incorporated

• Wong Enterprises

COMPANY

B   Listen again and complete the notes in the business trip schedule below.

SCHEDULE	AM	PM
Monday	• [＿＿＿] to airport at 8 a.m. • Check in at [＿] a.m. • Flight leaves at 11 a.m.	• Check in to Harbor Hotel • Meet Mr. Jiang in hotel [＿＿＿] at 6 p.m. Then [＿＿＿] dinner
Tuesday	• [＿＿＿]	• Meeting with Ms. Kumar from 3 p.m. to [＿] p.m. • US-style dinner with Mr. Stratton (met last [＿＿＿] in New York)
Wednesday	• [＿] a.m. taxi to venue • Meet guide, Ms. Lee, at venue's [＿＿＿]	• [＿＿＿] until 5 p.m.
Thursday	• Buy gifts for wife & children (and [＿＿＿])	• Depart Hong Kong at [＿] p.m.

76

I Have 22 Million Followers
—Social Media and News Stories

- **What are some merits and demerits of social media?**
- **Which types of news stories interest you? Why?**

Vocabulary Start!

Check the meanings of the words in the box below. Then choose the most appropriate answers for 1–8, and write them using the correct form.

1. Do you know what is _____ on social media this week?

2. That low-quality magazine only contains _____ about the lives of celebrities.

3. _____ the Internet for a long time every day is not good for your eyes.

4. Why do some countries heavily _____ the reporting by their media?

5. Today, an American _____ was injured while reporting on the war.

6. We're considering what specific _____ to include on our new website.

7. _____ often uses big, sensational _____ to sell more newspapers.

8. This newspaper _____ says that six _____ saw the accident.

headline	gossip	trending	the press	article
censor	journalist	browse	bystander	information

S Speeches: Headlines!

Listen to six news headlines and fill in the missing words in each headline.

1. TOKYO STOCK EXCHANGE _____
   ALL-TIME HIGH OF _____!

2. NEW PICTURE BY BRITISH ARTIST,
   PRANKSY, APPEARS INSIDE _____

3. _____ LIGHTS IN SKY—UFOs
   SPOTTED BY _____ IN MIAMI

4. 2 MILLION _____ FOUND
   IN SPORTS BAG UNDER _____
   STATION BENCH

5. ICEBERG THE SIZE OF A SMALL _____
   FLOATING IN NORTH ATLANTIC _____

6. ROBOT WITH ARTIFICIAL _____
   WINS _____ COMPETITION

Listening Tip

Weak Forms: Vowel Sounds ➡ Schwa

When words (especially short words) are not stressed, their vowel sounds can become weak and change to the "schwa" sound, /ə/.

Example | My grandmother used social media **for the** first time today!
➡ My grandmother used social media **fə thə** first time today

Practice ▷ Listen and write the words you hear in each blank space.

1. Do you want _____ write _____ blog?

2. Please sit _____ _____ back of the studio.

3. Could I interview you _____ _____ news program?

4. Put this photo on the right side _____ _____ page.

5. Can you e-mail me by 10 _____ _____ morning?

6. The thief stole _____ painting around 11 _____ night.

S News Stories: Headline News!

A   Listen to five news stories and match each one with the correct headline.

Story No. 1 •
Story No. 2 •
Story No. 3 •
Story No. 4 •
Story No. 5 •

• **Big, Beautiful Creature**
• **An Accidental Discovery**
• **Flying Through Water!**
• **A Rich Thief?**
• **Spectacle in the Sky**

B   Listen to the news stories again and write a short answer for each question.

Story No. 1

• What was stolen from the hotel?   _____

• Who searched the luggage?   _____

Story No. 2

• What will people be able to see tonight?   _____

• How often does the phenomenon occur?   _____

Story No. 3

• What new species was found in the Amazon jungle?   _____

• How large are its wings?   _____

Story No. 4

• What did the Taiwanese person ride?   _____

• What was the height of the new world record?   _____

Story No. 5

• What were the couple in the Caribbean for?   _____

• What did they accidentally find in the sand?   _____

Short Responses

Listen to each question or statement and circle the correct response to it.

1. **a.** Yes, it's an interesting article.
   b. No, but my parents do.
   c. Actually, I read it this morning.

2. **a.** Keeping in touch with friends.
   b. Mass media is very powerful.
   c. To be a sociable person is easy.

3. **a.** Without a doubt.
   b. No, it isn't really true.
   c. Yes, you can believe it.

4. **a.** In that case, shall we stay home?
   b. Yes, it was nice today, wasn't it?
   c. Then let's go to an outdoor pool.

5. **a.** Yes, I can.
   b. No, which one?
   c. Maybe I will.

6. **a.** To report on different lifestyles.
   b. To enjoy dangerous places.
   c. To let people know the facts.

[S] News Reports: What Type of Report?

A Listen to six news reports and number them in the order you hear them.

- [ ] Business News
- [ ] International News
- [ ] Sports News
- [ ] Domestic News
- [ ] Travel News
- [ ] Weather News

B Listen again and write a short answer to each question.

1. Which route is not running smoothly? _____

2. How much will a new passport cost? _____

3. What will the temperature be in the afternoon? _____

4. Where did the leaders meet? _____

5. What did Tom Link win in the long jump event? _____

6. What was the stock market's index figure this morning? _____

S Speeches: Introductions from Influencers

Listen to introductions from four influencers and circle T for *True* or F for *False*.

1. Mr. Me writes about special things in his daily life.   T   F
2. Mr. Me has 40 million followers who read his blogs.   T   F
3. Mara X teaches people how to select and put on make-up.   T   F
4. Mara X also sells the newest cosmetics to her followers.   T   F
5. Sam the Storyteller makes podcasts of stories he writes.   T   F
6. Sam the Storyteller's stories have different durations.   T   F
7. Cassy the Cookbook teaches about cooking in the home.   T   F
8. Cassy the Cookbook has 80.5 million followers.   T   F

M Conversation: Two Different Versions

Listen to Jack talking to his boss and fill in his version of an accident.

	Social Media Version	Jack's Version
Where was the accident?	Broad Street	
What vehicle was involved?	large truck	
What was spilled on the road?	oil	
Who was injured?	woman on bicycle	
What part of their body?	arm	
How many police officers came?	four	
In how many cars?	one	
What happened in the end?	started raining	

M Interview: Lottery Win!

A Listen to the first part of an interview from a news program and circle the correct answer to each question.

1. Where are Simon and Linda from?
   a. Buffalo
   b. Boston
   c. Baltimore

2. What is their relationship?
   a. Both single
   b. Engaged
   c. Married

3. What is Linda's job at the supermarket?
   a. Stock clerk
   b. Cashier
   c. Bagger

4. What does Simon's factory process?
   a. Food
   b. Garbage
   c. Chemicals

5. In which part of the city is their apartment?
   a. The center
   b. The south side
   c. The suburbs

6. How many bedrooms does their apartment have?
   a. One
   b. Two
   c. Three

7. What floor do they live on?
   a. First
   b. Second
   c. Third

8. What kind of food do they mainly buy?
   a. Domestic
   b. Discounted
   c. Imported

B Listen again and circle T for *True* or F for *False*, NG for *Not Given*.

1. Simon and Linda won $10 million in this year's biggest lottery.	T	F	NG
2. After getting married, they went on an inexpensive honeymoon.	T	F	NG
3. They lead lives that are quite complex and difficult.	T	F	NG
4. Their apartment building was constructed over a hundred years ago.	T	F	NG
5. Controlling the room temperature is a seasonal problem for them.	T	F	NG
6. They live between neighbors who are very loud.	T	F	NG
7. On a vacation last year, they bought many kinds of clothes.	T	F	NG
8. Simon sometimes brings unsaleable food home from his workplace.	T	F	NG

You're in Good Shape!
—Health and Wellbeing

- **Do you do anything to stay physically healthy?**
- **What do you do to take care of your mental health?**

Vocabulary Start!

Check the meanings of the words in the box below. Then choose the most appropriate answers for 1–8, and write them using the correct form.

1. When I stood up on the train, I felt very _____.

2. My younger brother had a very high _____, 38.8 degrees, in fact.

3. The doctor wrote me a _____ for some cold medicine.

4. The woman's hand was _____ because of the insect bite.

5. I have a _____ once a year, usually in spring.

6. After touching the plant, a _____ appeared on my skin.

7. When I _____, I shared a room with three other _____.

8. After the _____ on my stomach, I got an _____ that took weeks to heal.

fever	patient	prescription	infection	dizzy
operation	swollen	health check-up	be hospitalized	rash

83

M Speech: A Patient's Details

Listen to a nurse talking to a patient and complete the details on the form.

N NUTRO CLINIC

PRE-MEDICAL CHECK-UP FORM

Patient: *Gina Crawford*   Weight: _____ kilos

Gender: _____   Temperature: _____ degrees Celsius

Age: _____   Heart rate: _____ beats per minute

Height: _____ cm   Blood pressure: _____/_____

Listening Tip

Helping Sounds: "r, w, y"

When a word ends in a vowel sound and the next word begins with a vowel sound, sometimes an "r, w, y" sound is inserted between the words to make them easier to say.

| Example | The bab**y a**te the food and smiled. ➡ The baby **y**ate the food and smiled.

Practice ▶ Listen and circle the helping sound you hear in (r w y).

1. You (r w y) always look so healthy!

2. Judy (r w y) and her mother are at the hospital.

3. Would you like some vanilla (r w y) ice cream?

4. I often drink herbal tea (r w y) on my balcony.

5. How (r w y) are your parents, today?

6. How was the health and nutrition course? Did you enjoy (r w y) it?

S Conversations: Hospital Talk

Listen to five short conversations at a hospital and fill in each blank space with one word. The sentences (Person A, Person B) are taken from the conversations.

1. **B** You'll be fine in a day or two. Here's a _____ for some medicine.

   B Good. Make sure you take the _____ after each meal of the day.

2. **B** No, I'm fine, thank you. I'm just waiting for a _____.

   B Yes, the _____ assistant is bringing one for me now.

3. **A** Have you ever been a _____ of this hospital?

   A Okay. Could I see your _____ insurance card, please?

4. **A** Hello, _____ services. What's the problem?

   A Okay. I'll send an _____ there immediately.

5. **A** Excuse, me. I'm a little bit lost. Could you tell me how to get to _____ 6, please?

   A Yes, my aunt. She had an _____ yesterday.

M Conversations: Ailments & Treatments

Listen to a doctor who is seeing four patients and complete the notes in the chart.

PATIENT	AILMENT	CAUSE	DIAGNOSIS	TREATMENT
1. Joe Foster	☐ hurts, can't swallow anything	singing at a ☐ last night	☐	antibiotics
2. Milly Grant	backache, ☐ to lie down	carrying ☐ up and down stairs	slipped disk	☐
3. Carlos Garcia	ringing in ☐	listening to loud music on ☐	tinnitus	wear a ☐ aid
4. Mai Saito	itchy ☐, sneezing	tree pollen	☐	antihistamine eye ☐

85

L Conversation: A Heath Check-Up

Listen to a nutritionist talking to a patient and circle the correct answer to each question.

1. What is Mr. Goodman's occupation?
   a. Interior designer
   b. Graphic designer
   c. Web page designer

2. How much does he weigh?
   a. 70 kilos
   b. 80 kilos
   c. 90 kilos

3. How old is he?
   a. 26   b. 36   c. 46

4. How much should he weigh?
   a. 65 kilos   b. 70 kilos   c. 75 kilos

5. How often does he eat a sandwich and have coffee for breakfast?
   a. Sometimes
   b. Usually
   c. Never

6. How often does he eat cereal or drink fruit juice for breakfast?
   a. Almost never
   b. Almost always
   c. Sometimes

7. What does he usually have for lunch?
   a. Fish burger and fries
   b. Chicken burger and fries
   c. Hamburger and fries

8. How often does he cook and eat fresh salads or vegetables?
   a. Sometimes   b. Very rarely   c. Never

9. How many minutes does he walk each day to work?
   a. 5   b. 10   c. 20

10. How many cigarettes does he smoke per day?
    a. 10   b. 20   c. 30

Short Responses

Listen to each statement or question and circle the correct response to it.

1. a. It's nice to see you, too, doctor.
   b. I think I'll be fine in a moment.
   c. I'm a little bit tired and dizzy.

2. a. Twice a day is not enough.
   b. Okay, so after each meal.
   c. I tried that several times.

3. a. What did you eat this morning?
   b. Did you have a fight with someone?
   c. You look fine, so you can go home.

4. a. Yes, thank you.
   b. Yes, all the time.
   c. Yes, I know that.

5. a. Is this really the right way?
   b. Why? Where are we going?
   c. Mary's doing it right now.

6. a. I can carry different things.
   b. How long will the surgery last?
   c. Please don't touch me.

M Podcast: Relaxation Time ...

A Listen to a radio podcast and check ☑ the words you hear in the program.

C 73

| Mountain Forest |

☐ flowers   ☐ trees   ☐ animals   ☐ birds   ☐ butterflies   ☐ green plants

| Tropical Beach |

☐ waves   ☐ mind   ☐ palm trees   ☐ fish   ☐ white sand   ☐ coconuts

B Listen to the podcast again and circle the correct answer for each blank space.

C 73

1. Listeners should sit in a _____ chair.
   a. portable
   b. comfortable
   c. foldable

2. They should imagine they are in a forest and can hear a _____ nearby.
   a. lake
   b. waterfall
   c. river

3. They should breathe in the _____ forest air and hold their breath for three seconds.
   a. cool
   b. fresh
   c. fragrant

4. On the beach, they can feel a cool _____ over their body.
   a. breeze
   b. freeze
   c. tease

5. They should feel the ocean water touching their _____.
   a. hair
   b. fingers
   c. toes

6. The listeners' minds should feel relaxed and _____.
   a. empty
   b. calm
   c. open

A Listen to a conversation and write a short answer for each question.

C 74

1. When is Mr. Tong going to the hospital? _____

2. What are Oliver and Kelly going to do later this year? _____

3. When did Kelly have an operation at the hospital? _____

4. What part of the body was the operation on? _____

5. How is Mr. Tong going to travel to the hospital? _____

6. What will the hospital parking lots be like when Mr. Tong visits? _____

B Listen to the conversation again and complete the notes.

C 74

Millbank Hospital
_____

• Visiting hours: 10 a.m. to _____, 2 to ___ p.m.

• Kelly _____

• ward _____

• _____ wing

• _____ floor

• Parking lots by _____ and _____ wings

• Mr. Tong to arrive at about _____ o'clock

• Fairway Boulevard parking lot: ____ minutes
  from hospital

You Won't Catch Any Fish!
—Earth and the Environment

- **How do you think Earth's environment will be different in 50 years?**
- **In your daily life, what do you do to help protect the environment?**

Vocabulary Start!

Check the meanings of the words in the box below. Then choose the most appropriate answers for 1–8, and write them using the correct form.

1. The _____ in various parts of the planet are very fragile.

2. From the air, it is easy to see the _____ of the Amazon jungle.

3. Do you think many animals will become _____ in the near future?

4. Air _____ is a big problem in major cities around the world.

5. Wind, water, and sunlight are great sources of _____ energy.

6. Due to heavy _____ last week, many roads are still under water.

7. Because of _____ , we are experiencing _____ more frequently.

8. _____ is often buried in a _____ and is dangerous to people's health.

pollution	landfill	global warming	ecosystem	extinct
renewable	flooding	toxic waste	deforestation	drought

M Lecture: How Much Waste?

Listen to a professor talking about waste and fill in the missing information in the graph.

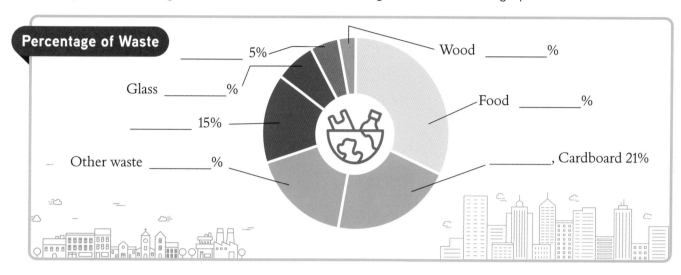

Percentage of Waste

_____ 5%

Glass _____ %

_____ 15%

Other waste _____ %

Wood _____ %

Food _____ %

_____, Cardboard 21%

Listening Tip

Shared Sounds: Last Consonant + First Consonant

When a word ends in a consonant sound and the next word begins with the same consonant sound, the sound is said only once, so it is "shared."

| Example | One urgen**t t**ask is to stop global warming!
➡ One urgen_**t**ask is to stop global warming!

Practice ▶ Listen and write two words with a shared sound in each blank space. (The shared sound is shown for each sentence.)

1. More people should _____ in their yards! (t)

2. It's a very _____ today, isn't it? (d)

3. We _____ swim in the lake because it's clean. (n)

4. Although it's a _____, it's very polluted. (s, c)

5. The _____ a long time to clear away. (t)

6. I use the _____ because buses are eco-friendly. (s)

7. The _____ of the mountain has a lot of snow on it. (p)

8. You need a _____ to cut down trees here. (l)

S Reports: Natural Disasters!

Listen to seven short reports related to weather and try to write the key word that is repeated (said two times) in each report.

Number 1	_____		Number 5	_____
Number 2	_____		Number 6	_____
Number 3	_____		Number 7	_____
Number 4	_____

Short Responses

Listen to each statement and circle the correct response to it.

1. a. It must be the heat.
   b. Do they need some water?
   c. How do you know?

2. a. Right, I'll remind you later.
   b. Oh, it's so dark in here.
   c. Don't worry. I won't.

3. a. I don't have a bicycle.
   b. I couldn't agree more.
   c. Where's the trash can?

4. a. Everyone should try it.
   b. Don't drink any more!
   c. It's not easy when it's cold.

5. a. They have beautiful leaves.
   b. I love climbing them.
   c. Why did they do that?

6. a. I'm up for that!
   b. I washed it earlier.
   c. It's already clear, isn't it?

M Conversation: Pollution & Opinions

Listen to two people discussing pollution stories in a newspaper and complete each blank space in the chart with one word.

POLLUTION TYPE	CAUSE: GEORGE'S OPINION	CAUSE: JILL'S OPINION
1. _____	_____ at night	_____'s loud music
2. _____	factory _____	acid _____
3. _____	garbage from the _____	_____

M Talk: "Fishing" in Amsterdam

Listen to someone describing an unusual activity in Europe and circle the correct answer to each question.

1. Amsterdam is the _____ of the Netherlands.
   a. shame
   b. dirtiest
   c. capital
   d. industry

2. The city is famous for its _____.
   a. waterways
   b. pathways
   c. expressways
   d. walkways

3. On a canal boat ride, you will catch _____.
   a. fish
   b. garbage
   c. oysters
   d. shellfish

4. Participants on the boats use _____.
   a. rods
   b. poles
   c. nets
   d. ropes

5. What is the main purpose of the boat rides?
   a. To take photos of Amsterdam
   b. To clean the canals
   c. To measure the garbage in the water
   d. To report different types of waste

6. The collected waste is _____ on the boats.
   a. counted
   b. sorted
   c. burned
   d. shredded

7. The activity stops the waste from going into the _____.
   a. city
   b. lake
   c. ground
   d. ocean

8. How many bags of all plastic can be gathered in one trip?
   a. two
   b. three
   c. five
   d. seven

9. What are recycled PET bottles used to make?
   a. tables and chairs for businesses
   b. cups and plates for local restaurants
   c. furniture for parks and gardens
   d. containers for modern offices

10. What else are recycled PET bottles used to make?
    a. floats
    b. boats
    c. taverns
    d. caverns

L Conversation: What Garbage? What Day?

Part 1   Listen to a conversation and circle T for *True* or F for *False*.

1. The neighbors' regular garbage is collected three times a week.   T   F
2. Burnable trash is picked up every Monday, Wednesday, and Saturday.   T   F
3. The large brown trash container is for waste that can be burned.   T   F
4. Non-burnable waste is taken away every 1st and 3rd Thursday.   T   F
5. The yellow trash container is for waste like glass and metal.   T   F
6. The neighbors should put waste for recycling in the blue trash container.   T   F
7. Recyclable waste is taken away two times a month.   T   F

Part 2 Listen as the conversation continues and circle the correct answer to each question.

1. What doesn't the new tenant want to keep?
  a. A chair
  b. A table
  c. A sofa

2. How should he contact the recycling center?
  a. By phone
  b. By e-mail
  c. Go there directly

3. When does the center pick up large waste items?
  a. In the morning
  b. In the afternoon
  c. In the evening

4. What is the pick-up cost based on?
  a. The pick-up time
  b. The size and weight
  c. The waste's condition

5. If he takes waste to the center himself, when must he contact the center before going there?
  a. 72 hours before
  b. 48 hours before
  c. 24 hours before

6. If he takes waste to the center himself, how much does he have to pay?
  a. A small charge
  b. Nothing
  c. He can decide

L Radio Program: Tips for Saving Resources

Part 1 Listen to the first part of a radio show where someone is giving advice on how to save resources and circle T for *True*, F for *False*, or NG for *Not Given*.

1. The host is talking with Alice Young from the Green, Clean Living Society. T F NG

2. Alice is offering advice on how to reduce our usage of gas in the home. T F NG

3. Her advice is to set air conditioners at 78 degrees Fahrenheit. T F NG

4. Fridges take 10 minutes to become cool again if you leave their doors open. T F NG

Part 2 Listen as the show continues and match the items in the three columns.

What People Should or Should Not Do

1. Don't leave • • shower heads • • every day.
2. Turn off • • bathtubs • • from faucets.
3. Take showers • • laundry • • than 10 minutes.
4. Only fill • • water dripping • • to around half.
5. Don't do • • for no longer • • properly.

Listen to someone asking two people, Andy and Kaya, questions about the environment.
Color in ● Andy's answers and <u>underline</u> Kaya's answers.

Q1. How concerned are you about the environment?
  ○ Very concerned   ○ Quite concerned   ○ Slightly concerned ○ Not concerned

Q2. How frequently do you recycle products?
  ○ Always   ○ Usually   ○ Sometimes   ○ Never

Q3. Have you ever had a health problem related to pollution?
  ○ Yes   ○ No   ○ Maybe   ○ Don't know

Q4. What do you think is the worst environmental problem today?
  ○ Air pollution   ○ Global warming
  ○ Water pollution   ○ Deforestation
  ○ Toxic waste   ○ Ozone depletion

Q5. Who do you think causes the most damage to our environment?
  ○ Governments   ○ Industry   ○ Individual people

Q6. Who should lead in taking action to solve environmental problems?
  ○ Governments   ○ Individual people
  ○ Industry   ○ Environmental groups

Q7. What do you think is the best solution for saving the environment?
  ○ Governments should make new economic policies to minimize pollution.
  ○ Companies that pollute the environment should be shut down.
  ○ Finding new technology that can solve environmental issue.
  ○ Get people to recycle more and use energy resources more efficiently .

Q8. Do you know what SDGs stand for?
  ○ Sustainable Development Goals
  ○ Sustainably Discarded Garbage
  ○ Suitable Developed Goals

                                    Thank you for taking part in this survey.